THIS IS THE F#$%ING NEWS

THIS IS THE F#$%ING NEWS

PADDY GOWER

with Eugene Bingham

MY STORY

ALLEN&UNWIN
AUCKLAND • SYDNEY • MELBOURNE • LONDON

First published in 2024

Images in the picture section are from the author's private collection, unless otherwise specified.

Allen & Unwin
Level 2, 10 College Hill, Freemans Bay
Auckland 1011, New Zealand
+64 (9) 377 3800
auckland@allenandunwin.com
www.allenandunwin.co.nz

83 Alexander Street
Crows Nest NSW 2065, Australia
+61 (2) 8425 0100

A catalogue record for this book is available from the National Library of New Zealand.

ISBN 978 1 991006 84 4

Design by Kate Barraclough
Cover photograph by Stephen Tilley
Wardrobe by Workshop
Printed and bound in Australia by the Opus Group

3 5 7 9 10 8 6 4 2

FSC www.fsc.org MIX Paper | Supporting responsible forestry FSC® C001695

For Mum, I'm gutted you missed all this.
(And apologies for the swearing.)

CONTENTS

1.
IT ALL STARTED IN A LIBRARY

It all began with just five words: This. Is. The. Fucking. News. The moment my career veered off in a direction I could not control. When I transformed from a political editor in a suit yapping at Parliament to a viral meme swearing in a library (still in a suit). It was a moment viewed millions and millions of times.

I've still got no idea where it came from, or why I did it. At the time, I definitely had no idea of the impact it would have. Whatever it was, snapping 'This is the fucking news!' in front of a camera in 2014 changed everything. And even now, ten years later, someone will come up to me and say it, or shout it across the street, pretty much every day. Yes, every fucking day. I'll be walking along the street, and someone will stop, stare, point and say: 'It's the Fucking News guy.' That's all they'll say — and then they'll just stare.

It has been printed on T-shirts, used on coffee mugs, there have even been artworks. I've seen a set of fine china dinner plates with a beautiful scene of a pond and 'This is the Fucking News' in fancy lettering. And at least two people have had it tattooed on them, alongside a rather large caricature of my face. (Please do not try this at home.)

I've been tagged into it on social media as it has gone round and round the internet. I can't get over how it's found an everlasting viral life, and how many people think it really was a blooper from the actual news. (For the record, it was a skit gone wrong, but I gave up bothering to explain that long ago.)

When it happened, I was coming up to my first election as political editor for *3News*. A lot of people were saying I didn't have what it took to do the job, that I was too much of a clown. I was actually trying to be more serious, and have some — fancy-word alert — 'gravitas'. Then I got a phone call, asking me to come along to the library at the Auckland Law School.

”

The true beginning of 'This is the Fucking News' was a different phrase — 'This is bloody exciting!' It was 2011 and I hadn't been on the telly for long. I was at SkyCity in Auckland on election night covering National leader John Key's party as the results rolled in. It was classic election-night coverage; the studio crossed to each party headquarters and asked a reporter: 'So, what's happening there?'

John Campbell was running the cutter from the studio, and he crossed to me standing with a group of Young Nats. Now, people who've seen any Young Nats know they have a very distinct look about them: young (obviously), very clean-cut, nerdy, a bit geeky. This group was clearly high on the drug known as Key-is-getting-a-second-term. As my live camera came on, I said to them something like, 'How are ya feeling about tonight?'

The nerdy, geeky guy in the centre, who'd clearly had a couple of fizzy wines, pushed forward, cracked a kooky smile and kind of lifted off, saying very loudly and very funnily, 'This is bloody exciting!' It was a crack-up moment and afterwards he cleverly pushed it out on social media.

The kid was called Sean Topham. It was no surprise he became the Young Nats head honcho after that, and I'd see him around the political traps. (I should note here that he's gone on to have a successful international career in social media and is something of a global force, known for his ability to conjure up viral content for political campaigns. Given what he was about to get me into, it makes a hell of a lot of sense.) In August 2014, Sean got in touch about this idea for the Auckland Law Revue, a production put on every year by law students from the University of Auckland. Various luminaries of the New Zealand legal scene have been involved over the years and it was always a laugh, as well as a bit controversial. It started as a stage show, but a year earlier, part of the performance had migrated online with a feminist response to 'Blurred Lines', the Robin Thicke video featuring naked women — and it had gone viral globally. So Sean said, 'You know the "Blurred Lines" video?'

'Yeah, yeah,' I replied.

'This year, we're going to do a spoof of the Kevin Spacey American political drama, *House of Cards*.'

I was listening. I fucking loved that programme.

'We've got this plotline,' said Sean, 'where two people are

trying to become president of the Law Society, and there's a journalist investigating them. And we need a journalist to play the role.' I was hooked because, despite my quest for 'gravitas', I was constantly tempted by anything that involved clowning around. I couldn't resist; I was already visualising myself in this viral spoof. And then Sean said, 'I was wondering if you could ask John Campbell or give me his number. Any help would be appreciated and bloody exciting!' What a let-down: they wanted JC and not me. This wasn't bloody exciting at all.

But I said, 'Yeah, alright, I'll get hold of Campbell.' So I passed on an email invite from Sean. A week later, Sean asked if I'd do it instead. I texted back: 'Has Campbell rejected you?'

'Haven't heard from him . . .'

That would teach him. 'Hahahaha,' I messaged.

'Haha . . . please?' he replied.

Most people would've said 'Nah, I'm busy', or something. But of course, forgetting about gravitas, forgetting about pride, and thinking a lot about clowning around, I texted back: 'K. When?' It may be relevant that this text was sent well after midnight. It was more than likely I'd had a few to drink.

”

A few days later, we were in the law library filming this thing. Now, libraries and I have always had a 'complicated' relationship. Back in the day, I was a big reader and I'd rack up a lot of overdue fines, which my Old Lady would have to pay so I could get out more books. And then, when I was at school, I terrorised our school librarian, Mrs Gaffney, and faced bans for various breaches of library protocol. So maybe a law library wasn't the best place for me, but I wasn't thinking that when these young students wandered in with a small camera and not much other equipment. It didn't look very professional. Boy, I underestimated them.

We were filming a scene where I was doing a live cross about the presidential race between two characters, James and Phoebe. We were riffing and mucking around with this skit. I was saying 'The campaign between James and Phoebe is really heating up', as if I was a political reporter breaking down the battle for law-school president. We were just making it up as we went along, and the idea was that someone in the library would stand up and interrupt me, saying, 'This is a fucking library.' I was supposed to just reply, 'Shhhhhhh.'

But I changed it up and fired back: 'This is the fucking news.' I don't know why, it just came out. Everybody in the library cracked up. Obviously the joker in me enjoyed that. I have to admit, I walked out of that library a teeny bit worried about what would come of it. But I was thinking, *It's just a little skit, it'll go away.* So off I went back to the election campaign trail and forgot about it.

"

A few weeks later, I got a text from Sean explaining that everyone thought the 'This is the fucking news' line was funny but it didn't really fit with the overall *House of Cards* parody.

I was relieved, glad it was going to disappear. Then Sean said they'd clipped it up separately. 'We're going to put it up on YouTube.'

Hmmmmm.

I texted him: 'Do you think it needs to be bleeped?'

'Nah, it's epic! Do you want it bleeped?'

'Let me think about it,' I replied.

You've got to remember this was a different time in my career — I was a political editor grappling for this elusive 'gravitas'. Bleeping it would probably have stopped things there and then. So you know what the response should have been, right? It should have been a hard yes to bleeping. Instead, not even a minute went by before I texted him back: 'Should be sweet.' *Should be sweet*: this thing was away.

Still, it took a while to land. It sat on YouTube for a while with just 162 views, at least twenty of them mine. I was on edge because those seemingly unprofessional students had put some fake *3News* graphics on it, and it looked real. So when it wasn't moving, I thought, *This is good. No one's noticing; the bosses will never find this.* A few months went by, I'd forgotten about it altogether, and then there was a pivotal intervention from a Kiwi guy called Dan Lake, aka Dan News, who made news-blooper collections from around the world — a weather guy from a local station in Tennessee gets blown over by the wind, that sort of thing.

For whatever reason — because remember, it wasn't a blooper, it was a skit — he put 'This is the Fucking News' in the blooper reel. And it looked legit, especially sandwiched between six or seven minutes of international bloopers. As soon as it went up, I started getting text messages from people saying, 'Hey, that blooper is hilarious.' I looked on YouTube and people were tagging the timecode in the comments and sharing it with people all over the world. I thought, *This is not good.* By that night, I was pretty worried and wondered whether I should give the bosses a heads-up. But it was late, so I left it and went to bed.

When I woke up in the morning, my phone had blown up. People everywhere were messaging and tagging me on social media. While I'd been sleeping, it had been made into a meme by someone who'd clipped it out of Dan News's video and mixed it to rap music, with a close-up of my face at the end along with the caption 'thug life'. The viral video was called '*3News* Thug Life'. The whole thug-life meme came from the rapper Tupac Shakur, and was a humorous trend where the hardcore saying was applied to someone who was not that hardcore. It is hard to explain why the version with me in it took off, and it has been harder to find out who made it — they're out there somewhere. But it was picked up and shared by an early influencer, a Kiwi-Aussie rapper called Fortafy, who had a decent following. It went viral: one million views overnight.

I was shitting myself about what head of news Mark Jennings would say, and he was on the blower before I knew it, grumpy as. 'What happened here?' But the funny thing was, he didn't know what to do. 'What can we do? How can we stop it?' Neither of us had a clue.

The other Mark around at the time was Mark Weldon, the chief executive of MediaWorks, owner of TV3. After I hung up from Jennings, my phone rang again and it was Weldon. When I saw his number, I panicked. It was a very unpredictable era with him in charge and to receive a phone call from him directly was not good. I answered really gingerly. 'Ah . . . hello?' I didn't know what was going to happen. Was I going to get yelled at? Was I going to get fired?

But, immediately, Weldon told me he loved it, people were talking about it, and all he wanted to know was: 'How can we monetise it?'

'Um, sorry, what?' I was taken aback. At the time, the idea of monetising it seemed like a horrifying idea. I just wanted it to go away. At least Weldon wasn't grumpy like Jennings. Sitting where I am today, I do have the odd pang of regret. Yeah, why didn't we monetise it? Why didn't *I* monetise it?

The truth was I still had no idea how big and out of control this was going to get, although I soon had a taste of what was to come. I was on holiday, walking along a quiet street in Wānaka on a sunny 28-degrees day, with my sunglasses on, having a nice chilled-out time. A car came along, a metallic purple lowered Holden with a bunch of teenagers in it — I could pretty much guarantee they were from Gore — and they clocked me as they went past. I saw the indicator go on, and next thing they were back around the block in front of me again. The car slowed right down and this kid poked his head out of the window, looked straight at me and yelled, 'This is the fucking news!' The whole car cracked up and skidded off. People were popping their heads out of their gardens, looking down the street at what was going on, and I was left dumbfounded by the whole scene. I remember thinking to myself, *This whole 'Fucking News' thing will die down by the end of summer.* Well, it never fucking died down.

Over the years, I'd try to distance myself from it. People would come up to me with their phone recording and go, 'Say it, Mister.' People would contact me, saying, 'My uncle really loves you. It's his fiftieth birthday, can you record a video? Please say: "This is Fucking Uncle Colin."'

For quite a few years, I would just never, ever say it, thinking, *I'm going to kill this off, I'm not going to put petrol on the fire.* So I'd tell people, 'Nah, I can't. My bosses hate me saying that.'

Kill it? That would actually make them crack up laughing. They'd be like, 'Really? That's so good!' So that just added to it. Because, as I said, there was this myth that it was a real blooper that I had said on the news. For the millionth time: It. Was. A. Skit. People would always want to know, 'Did you get in trouble for that?' I would try to play it down. Kill it, kill it, kill it. But things weren't helped by the invention of TikTok. It started in the era of Facebook and YouTube, then TikTok made it go viral around the world again. Eventually I realised, no matter what I did, I couldn't kill this thing. It was unkillable.

,,

Eventually I accepted that 'This is the Fucking News' was how lots of people knew me, like it or not. I have ended up taking a perverse kind of satisfaction in that. My journalism career has taken a very linear, steady approach — ten years at the *New Zealand Herald*, then the Parliamentary Press Gallery, *3News* political reporter, *3News/Newshub* political editor, moderating election debates, presenting documentaries and then my own show.

But despite all that work, I am best known for swearing in a library. I fucking love that.

I used to hate it. But over time I've accepted that, actually, it is a gift. Because it gives me a connection with people, young and old. They feel like they know me because of it. It opens people up to all the other important stories I want to tell, issues I investigate and things I want to say. It took me a long time to get to this point, but now I'm thankful I swore that day. I didn't want it to define me. But it does define me. And I'm all good with that.

I'm the Fucking News guy. And this is my story.

2.
BACKYARD NINJA

The garden of my childhood home, or 'down the back' as I called it, is one of my most special places. To get down there, you have to cross the deck my parents built onto the back of the house. That deck is full of memories, too. It's where Mum and Dad (or 'The Olds' as I call them) took in the news I'd landed my first job as a journalist. I still remember that like it was yesterday, even though it was 25 years ago. They were stoked — the Old Lady even got out the bubbles to celebrate. It was that special. A big day, with big things to come; bigger than any of us realised at the time.

The Old Man made an infamous speech on the deck at my twenty-first. He started all deadpan, then said something like, 'When Paddy was born the doctor came out and said, "It's an alien!"' My mates all cracked up. Dad's a funny bastard, I'll give him that. He loves his speeches, holding court with a few jokes. I always loved watching and listening to him. I did my yard glass that night on the lawn (I sculled my yardie in under two minutes, just saying). Nana, who was 80-something and five-foot-nothing, was cheering me on.

Under the deck was a pathway leading to the rest of the garden. Mum used to flick her cigarette butts down there. It still hurts to think about them lying around, even though the butts are long gone — because she is, too. The garden carried on with steps and levels right to the bottom, where a thin plank bridge crossed a creek beneath large trees; their branches hung like giant green arms wanting to wrap around me. The creek was small, but still big enough for eels. There was a big one that hung out at the neighbours' because they fed him sour cream. I always wanted to catch him, but I resisted. He was like their pet, so it would have been a bit stink. Believe it or not, I caught a tiny brown trout there once — by tickling it. It was about half a foot long. I'd read in a book about tickling trout, so one day I gave it a go — it fell asleep, and bang, I had it in my hands!

I was quite the nature lover as a kid. There were all sorts of birds in the garden and I was a keen amateur ornithologist. Very, very keen. I'd make little sketchbooks with facts about birds. And I always dreamt of finding a huia — an extinct native bird. Imagine that — the huia being rediscovered by a kid in a New Plymouth backyard! I had an incredible imagination; I was a backyard dreamer. I'd spend hours playing make-believe — mainly as a commando outwitting huge invading forces, or a ninja jumping around and taking out invisible enemies with hand-to-hand combat.

Anyone who's played make-believe knows the worst thing is to be seen or caught out. But down the back, it was so private, no one could see me. It was my own world, where I believed anything was possible.

,,

I was born at Taranaki Base Hospital on 1 April 1977, and, just for the record, the doctor said nothing at all about me being an alien. It was April Fool's Day, so read into that what you will. My parents, Joan and Gordon, had moved up to New Plymouth from Christchurch when Dad got a job at the power station, which as a kid I just knew as the big chimney down by the port. He'd work night shifts, riding off on his ten-speed bike in his white overalls.

In the late 1980s, he got a new pair of overalls, maroon with 'Electricorp' written on them. They looked a lot flasher than his old white pair to me, but the Old Man wasn't happy. 'These bastards,' he'd say. I was confused — but of course he was talking about the 1980s Rogernomics reforms that created state-owned enterprises like Electricorp from the New Zealand Electricity Department. Dad was a staunch Labour man who'd been a member of the party before he could vote, and he was a staunch union man, too. Of course he felt betrayed by Labour ministers Roger Douglas and Richard Prebble, who were pursuing a right-wing economic agenda.

Dad was a fitter and turner by trade; his work was fixing and operating machinery. He was also into politics — he'd learnt it in the workplace — and he'd talk about it at home all the time. So I picked up a bit of kitchen-table politics along with all his banter, too.

My mum was a quiet lady. Even though she had left school

early, she was really brainy, and had educated herself by reading heaps of books. She liked writing, too; I have some poems she wrote as a kid. She worked as a receptionist for the local doctors when I was growing up and was really empathetic, so lots of people would confide in her. She'd have lots of visitors come round home, friends and acquaintances who were going through troubles, and they'd be outside talking to Mum while she was smoking, sharing their secrets and getting advice. One of Mum's greatest traits was that she never judged anyone, something I would try to emulate later in life.

Mum and Dad were both immigrants; Dad arrived in New Zealand when he was a baby, and Mum when she was about ten. They both grew up in working-class families — Mum in Manurewa, South Auckland, and Dad in Kaiapoi, north of Christchurch. Their parents came here for the Kiwi dream, to get a better life for their children and the generations after that. Which included, of course, yours truly, me — Patrick James Gower.

"

I reckon we can learn a lot about ourselves from who we come from. My dad was a Pom; he was born in London. His mother, my grandmother, was called Bertha, a great name. I never got to know her, as she died when I was three months old, knocked off her bike by a car. She'd been in London when it was getting bombed during the Blitz in World War Two and came to New Zealand to be somewhere safe. She was apparently a real performer, writing plays and putting on skits for groups of women around Kaiapoi.

She was into fashion, and worked at a department store dressing well-to-do North Canterbury farmers' wives.

My grandfather George Gower was a seaman, born and raised in Portsmouth, England, and fought in both world wars. I never met him either; he died of cancer a week before I was born. He was on the RMS *Olympic* (the sister ship of the *Titanic*) during several daring skirmishes in World War One and won a medal for rescuing several men. He was an adventurous guy who travelled all over the world, and could play the piano, mouth organ and concertina as well as sing. Apparently, he'd light up pubs when he walked in, earning more coin from performing than he did on the boats.

”

Mum was born in London, too, but she was actually Irish. She still had an Irish-English accent when she got here, aged ten, and she was teased pretty badly. On my mum's side, my grandad, Joe Larkin, was from County Galway, and my nana, Brigid, was from County Donegal. Grandad Joe was an adventurous fella as well. Even though he was Irish and hated England and the King, he was keen to get off to World War Two. So he joined the Scots Guards, which was Scottish rather than English; apparently that made him feel better, and he ended up driving a tank around Egypt.

Like so many Irish at that time, he and Nana decided to leave the country and initially headed to London, where my mum and her sister were born. Grandad's first job in New Zealand was painting the Auckland Harbour Bridge. He spent most of his life as a labourer. I didn't get to know him that well before he died, mainly because I couldn't understand his thick Irish accent.

I knew my Nana Brigid the best. She'd worked in sewing factories around South Auckland. She hadn't had much formal education back in Ireland, but she could speak Gaelic and was always reading. She was very interested in international affairs and had a really detailed atlas full of all sorts of information about different countries. I'd talk to her a lot. I know she never really felt at home in New Zealand and always missed Ireland and her sisters scattered all around the world — coming here meant missing out on a lot.

In her later years, I'd go and see Nana in her retirement unit, and take clippings of my stories from the *New Zealand Herald* to leave with her to read. She was really proud, like I'd made the All Blacks.

I hope in some way it made her think all those sacrifices were worth it. If I could say something to my grandparents, that would be it. Thanks for bringing us here. I hope my life is what you dreamt of.

”

I was always a bit of a hard-case little bastard. I can remember once a kid at school called me a 'poof', as in poofter, which was slang for homosexual. I had no idea what he was talking about, so I came home and looked it up in the dictionary. It said 'poof' was a small cushion for your feet, a footstool. So I went out and asked The Olds, 'Why am I being called a little footstool?' The Olds wanted to know more and I said, 'I've been called a poof.' They both roared with laughter. I didn't know why they were laughing, but I remember it felt cool to make them laugh.

It didn't take long for me to hit the media. I was only eleven when I landed on the front page of the local evening paper, the *Taranaki Herald*, after a school trip to the New Plymouth District Council. We were taken through to the mayoral chamber where we met the mayor, David Lean. The picture in the paper is of me with his robe and mayoral chains on looking at him and asking questions. I asked him why the water tasted so bad, and then, 'Where does your pay packet come from?' Talk about getting straight to the hard questions. The newspaper described it as a school trip turning into a coup against the mayor. It's pretty crazy looking back, knowing what was to come.

There was a radio appearance soon after, too, when a school camp went wrong. I was about twelve years old and we'd gone on a school trip on Taranaki Anniversary weekend, staying at Holly Hut up on the mountain. I was pretty fit and quick back in the day, and I was one of the first boys up to the hut. Then the rain started to pour. It was torrential. There was a dry riverbed outside the hut and I can remember looking at it and seeing brown mud hooning down. You could hear the rocks rolling in the riverbed. It was rain of Biblical proportions.

The teachers decided to get us out and back down the mountain. They spoke to a few of us and said some kids were going to have to stay behind because they were injured or sick, like one of my mates who had a sprained ankle. And they wanted a couple of us faster ones to stay back with them in case they needed to get a message out. I remember thinking, *This isn't good.* I wanted to get the hell out.

So most of the group headed off, while we stayed back in the hut. I was crying.

Next thing, all the boys were back — it was too rough to get across the river. So we were all trapped on Mount Taranaki, and ended up having to stay for a night or two. When we eventually got down, there was a radio journalist waiting in the car park because it was quite a big story. They were asking us what we thought, and some of the boys had a word or two to say. Then the microphone came to me and I was thinking about the food we'd had to make do with, so I said: 'The porridge tasted like crap.'

To the journalist, it would have been absolute gold. But the teachers must have been mortified because when we got back to school there were more reporters and a TV camera, and I remember the teachers saying, 'Keep Gower away.' My TV debut would have to wait.

❞

I went to St Joseph's Catholic School for my primary-school years, and had a proper Catholic upbringing — well, sort of. I clearly remember crying on my first day of school, mainly because I was shocked that Mum had to leave. I couldn't understand it. I quickly met some of the mates I'd have for life, and as I grew up there was a lot of fishing down at the wharf and off the breakwater, and a lot of eeling. My sporting career got off to an interesting start playing football; I was reserve goalkeeper, a sign of things to come on the athletic front.

Soon enough, me and some of the boys were off to high school at Francis Douglas Memorial College, which was just up the road. It was another Catholic school, and we'd sing hymns, say prayers, have religious education and go to Mass every week. They were really pushing the Catholicism, but not much stuck. My mum's parents were Catholic, and Mum took us to Mass on Sundays at St Joseph's Church. But Dad never came because apparently he was 'tired from work'. He'd only rev up for Mass once a year at Christmas, when he became this one-day-a-year churchgoer. Meanwhile us kids, who went every weekend, would be complaining about why we had to go to Mass on Christmas Day because it ruined the whole day. Every year it was the same fight.

Anyway, usually it was me, my younger sister and Mum, tucked on the end of a pew, beside the other families who would often have four, five or six kids — good Catholics. One of my best mates came from a family of eleven. When I was about seventeen and it was time for me to be confirmed — which is a special ceremony to affirm your commitment as a Catholic — I didn't want to do it. It wasn't a big revolt. I told Mum and then I said, 'I actually don't want to go to church anymore either.' And she stopped going to church, too. So that was it — after going this far, our staunch Catholicism just sort of ended with a whimper. We could have done it years earlier!

Yet clearly all those sermons got through deep down because I have retained many of the basic Catholic values I grew up with, like treating people how you want to be treated, being compassionate, and serving the community when you can. But obviously I don't believe any of that crap against abortion, homosexuality, or sex before marriage, and the church has a lot to answer for over all the abuse.

People can be a bit awkward talking about religion in New Zealand. I'm proud of my Catholic upbringing, and I believe in God — I think God is the love all around us. It's a very simple approach and it suits me. I still go to Mass every now and then, including every Christmas, mainly to remember Mum.

"

Mum and Dad were laid-back, good parents. No dramas. Go to work, love your kids, enjoy good times with your mates at the weekend. There were barbecues and parties most weekends, Dad sipping on white cans of Steinlager, Mum with Blenheimer wine casks or a Bacardi and Coke. The drinking wasn't like *Once Were Warriors* or anything — the scenes I remember from that time are more like an old-school alcohol ad, everyone in '80s clothing with a drink in hand. I guess if there was a family religion, this was it, as I certainly can't remember the Old Man missing a piss-up because he was 'tired from work'.

Every summer our family would pile in the car and drive up to Whitianga on the Coromandel Peninsula to meet up with my mum's family. Dad would drive through the night and us kids would sleep in the back. Nana and Grandad would be there, too, and my aunty, uncle and cousins. We'd go to the beach and eat sandwiches out of Tupperware containers. My cousins were older, so they were sort of heroes to me, like big brothers. At the end of the holiday, we'd pack up and head back to New Plymouth, back to normal life.

It was all good Kiwi stuff. We were living the dream. It was an idyllic childhood, my parents loved us heaps and that's all I really think of when I look back. Lots of love being around. But it didn't take long until I was really testing them with my larrikin streak.

After the teachers at primary school noticed I was being a bit of a smart-arse, Mum and Dad got called in to see the principal, who told them I should see a child psychologist. I can't remember much about the appointment, but Dad reckons the psychologist told them, 'There's nothing wrong with this boy — he's just bored.' His recommendation was that I be put up a class and all would be fine. And so I was moved forward a year. It meant I was one of the youngest and smallest kids in the class, but I still had one hell of a mouth on me — in more ways than one. And that was about to have big consequences at high school.

3. PADDY CARROTS

The thing with bullying is the lack of control. You have no power. You never know when someone is going to say something; you never know when someone is going to bring you down.

By the time I left primary school, I was smaller than other kids in my class. And I had massive buck teeth. My dad had an overbite and his nickname when he was younger was 'Smiley'. Genetics had handed me the overbite as well as big front teeth. At high school, I'd get called 'Bugsy' (as in Bugs Bunny), plain old 'Teeth', or the more personal 'Paddy Carrots'.

I hated it. Particularly when one of the older boys said it, because I looked up to them, and it made me feel different, as if I wasn't wanted. It would hurt much more than a punch. It just stripped away all my confidence. I remember being at a barbecue and an adult friend of the family said, 'I hear you get teased about those teeth, but they actually look strong and healthy.' She was trying to be nice, but I just loathed being singled out like that. I hated my teeth being mentioned in any way at all.

At school, I'd be playing handball or bouncing a ball in the quad with my mates and someone would yell something out about my teeth. Maybe they didn't realise what it did to me. Maybe they did. Who knows? But for me, all the fun, all the laughter would just drop away from that moment. It felt like all the colour was fading out of the world around me.

The teasing wasn't so bad that I was crying myself to sleep at night, and it's not like I stopped wanting to go to school. It certainly helped that my good mates never hassled me about it. The only nickname they ever gave me was 'PG'. I loved being called it then, and I still love it when people call me that now.

But from the age of ten, the teasing and name-calling about my teeth set in place this burden of being judged for the way I looked — a sensitivity about my looks, a weakness that stayed with me for decades.

I did what other bullied kids did: I buried stuff, I developed self-defences, I pretended it didn't hurt me. Yet even as an adult, with a successful career, becoming one of the most recognisable faces in the country, somewhere inside I was still the self-conscious little kid in the playground. And that would bring problems for me.

”

As I got older and hit puberty, I ended up with really bad acne — I had zits everywhere, not just on my face but also on my chest. Blackheads in the ears, whiteheads on the nose. You name it, I had it. It was so bad that I was put on the drug Roaccutane. Anybody who has been on this will know what a nightmare it is. It was very effective in my war against acne, but made my skin so dry it flaked so badly that it hurt to move my face.

Over time, I also ended up with braces and my facial features changed as well. I'd initially been this blond-haired, angelic-looking kid with normal teeth. But in my later teenage years, my hair turned dark and I had a big, oily, shiny nose. So with the buck teeth that came through, the braces, the acne, the dry skin, the big nose and the changing face shape, it was fair to say I had a lot going on.

In my later high-school years, a name came along that I really despised: 'Dog Face'. I *really* hated this one. It would completely take the wind out of me. The last time I can remember being called it was in my first year at Victoria University at one of the first really big nights out during Orientation Week. There were some guys there who'd been at New Plymouth Boys' High who knew me from back home, and one of them called out, 'Hey, Dog Face is at uni!' I just froze and thought, *Fuck*.

I'd been relatively lucky at school — Francis Douglas Memorial College wasn't like the yard at a maximum-security prison or anything. It was a smaller school and most people looked out for you. But I know there were kids who suffered much worse than me. There was a guy in my year who'd been born with some physical issues, so bad that he wasn't even meant to live. He had the absolute hell bullied out of him, and that's stuck with him. There were other kids, too. One of my friends was gay and he told me later that was hell for him.

I look back now and just wish I'd stuck up for others. But at the time, you're all just trying to survive. And so I never really said anything, putting my head down, desperately hoping no one would shout out 'Paddy Carrots'.

"

There came a day I thought my issues with my teeth were over. Painfully so. We were on holiday in Rotorua, and were at the pools. I was zooming down a famous hydroslide called The Black Hole; it was all dark and had these dips on the way down and you'd really get some air as you went over them.

I was shooting down one of the dips when my head whiplashed against the slide. White shards went flying and, sure enough, when I arrived at the bottom my front teeth were smashed to smithereens and all that was left looked like a couple of fangs. I was in a lot of pain and after a stop at the emergency doctors for some painkillers it was a long drive back to New Plymouth to see a dentist. I had my head in my Old Lady's lap all the way.

Before we got to the dentist, I remember Dad saying, 'Hopefully they can file them down a bit.'

I felt some relief. I was thinking, *Maybe I'll come out of this without buck teeth.* But of course it was a little more complex than that and the teeth were just capped, and weren't any smaller at all.

Although we didn't talk at home about the bullying, it must have been weighing on my parents' minds. They took me to an oral surgeon in Auckland to see if he could do anything. But it would have meant reconstructing my jaw with some major surgery, and it was going to break the family bank to pay for it. Instead, as Dad tells it now, they tried to let us know that to them, we were the best kids in the world. Dad says he and Mum talked about what they'd gone through as kids themselves — Dad with his buck teeth and Mum with her Irish accent — and how their own parents had instilled in them a sense of self-esteem. So that's what they decided to do with me. They made our home a sanctuary.

"

Like I say, the group of mates I became closest to were great, and we became really tight. And when I say tight, I mean tight as a cycling peloton, literally. There was a group of us boys from Francis Douglas Memorial College who met up each day to ride our bikes to school. Often there was a headwind, a really furious one, that would almost stop us when we turned into it.

So we'd all bunch up and someone would ride to the front and head into the wind for a while, then someone else would take a turn. It became tradition that whoever was at the front would be yelling and swearing at the wind, 'You bastard! You wanker!' It must have looked like a crack-up to anyone driving past, these kids yelling and cursing with their little helmets on.

One of the kids in the peloton was Conrad Smith, who went on to become an All Black. I was mates with his older brother. Even though he was younger than us, Conrad always took his turn at the front; he really was a tough little bugger. We'd also rope him into these big neighbourhood rugby-league games — two-on-two in the dead-ball area, first to 100 tries. They'd sometimes go for five hours. I've always said that was where Conrad learnt to tackle. He won't mind me saying that he was so competitive, he'd cry if things weren't going his way.

A lot of my mates were like that, too, hyper-competitive, and in the First XI cricket and First XV rugby teams. Not me. I was a fill-in for the Second XI, and in the Fourth XV. I was pretty small back then; I'm 6 foot 3 inches (1.9 metres) now, but I didn't shoot up until university.

Although I was relatively skilful and fit at school, I could never apply myself to anything. But in my final year, I did make it to House Captain of Benildus, a saint's name for the green house. I ran a mini-campaign to win the necessary votes, even though I was a bit of an underdog — my slogan was 'I'm no Yes Man'. This remains my one political campaign. We had our successes under my leadership. I was a good swimmer and led us to victory in the school swimming sports that year.

And there was a famous rugby moment. We were playing another house, Loreto, and it was all locked up in the final minutes. I was one-on-one with the First XV fullback, my mate Dion. I had players outside me, but I threw the most theatrical and outrageous dummy — Dion bought it and I scored under the posts for the win. It was a *Mighty Ducks* moment for the maverick Fourth XV captain against the star First XV fullback. Without doubt it was my finest sporting moment.

”

The values of courage and service were instilled in us at school, particularly because of Father Francis Douglas, who the college was named after when it opened in 1959. He was a Catholic priest who came up from Wellington to Taranaki to serve, and by all accounts he really got into the lifestyle, especially rugby and cricket.

Despite his love for the province, Father Francis had a calling to be a missionary and he headed overseas to the Philippines. Conditions were tough, made only worse and more dangerous when the Japanese invaded in 1942. Father Francis stayed on, and would sneak into the jungle to take confessions and say Mass to Filipino freedom fighters. The Japanese gave him a chance to leave, but he chose to remain and carry on his work. Eventually, the Japanese lost patience and accused him of being a spy. He was interrogated and there were demands he give people up and reveal secrets he'd been given during confession. Despite being beaten and tortured, he remained silent and refused to betray his vows. He was taken away and never seen again, and is believed to have been killed by the Japanese.

When I was at school, I didn't really take much notice of him or what he was about. His story didn't mean anything until after I left. But as life has gone on, Francis Douglas has become a hero of mine, because of the way he lived. He withstood pain and torture to protect his friends. His mahi, and looking after other people, was so important, he pushed on even if it meant losing his own life. Not many of us can say we live with such purpose.

So, if you take away the religion, I left school with the message of serving others — that was very much part of what we were taught. It's not like I walked out the school gate saying, 'Right, I'm off to serve.' But as I've got older, that idea of community service and purpose became really important to me, and that clearly started at Francis Douglas Memorial College. So I'd just like to say to all those teachers I made suffer: it wasn't all a waste of time.

”

I'm sure most teachers wondered what was going to become of me. To say I was a class clown would be putting it nicely. I was an absolute bloody nuisance. On the disruption scale, I was at the nuclear end. Probably the most trouble I got into was over the infamous 'dick bun' scandal.

Once a week, the boarders would be served saveloys for lunch, like hot dogs in a bun. We called them dick buns, for obvious reasons. One day in third form, only God knows why, I put one out through the zipper of my shorts, with cream from a doughnut on the end, and I walked across the yard. And again, only God knows why, I walked into the science lab where there were some guys in detention, with a teacher supervising.

Yeah, I got into quite a lot of shit for that. Mum and Dad had to come up to the school and the vibe in the principal's office wasn't particularly great as he outlined the facts. I couldn't really explain why I'd done it. It didn't look good, but I wasn't meaning to be perverted and I wasn't making any kind of statement. I was just out for a laugh. It certainly left a mark — guys from school still bring up the 'dick bun' escapade. It is one hell of a legacy.

I also got busted for what would have to be one of the earliest cases of computer hacking. The first real computers had come into the school and were set up in the library. This was back in 1992, when laptops were only a dream, and the computers were the size of a small house. I'd somehow figured out the teachers had very simple passwords — first name, last name — so I could get into their accounts. One lunchtime, a mate and I hacked the system; we could see the school reports that were due to come out, and we realised we could manipulate them. I was in one of my classmates' reports and was loudly and excitedly explaining how easy it would be to do him a solid and bump his grades up a bit. Big mistake.

On the other side of the thin wall was the assistant principal, 'Mr D'. He could hear everything. He stormed around to where we were, snuck up as I continued blathering on about how I was gonna make a lot of guys look more brainy, put his hand on the back of my neck and forced my head down onto the desk, next to the keyboard. 'Gotcha!' All hell broke loose. Mum and Dad were called up to the school again, and once again the vibe in the principal's office was not particularly great, and once again I couldn't really explain why I'd done it.

My antics weren't always deliberate. One time I came into economics and the teacher accused me of being late (I was) and I went to dramatically slam my bag down on my desk in protest. But it hooked on my finger as it flew out of my hand. I lost control of the bag; it was no longer heading to my desk, but instead towards the internal window between the classroom and the corridor. Bang! Smash! It shattered the window. Holy shit! I looked at the teacher and he was as shocked as me.

Every kid and teacher in the classrooms along the corridor raced out to see what the hell had happened. I just started walking for the door because I knew for sure I was going to get kicked out. I picked my bag up out of the broken glass and just kept walking — all the way home.

So there was a consistent pattern of being the clown, getting kicked out of class, and causing trouble, deliberately or not.

I remember when some All Blacks came to visit the school. This was a very big deal. We were all called to assembly and the All Blacks were on stage giving out prizes. Cans of Coke, that sort of thing. By this time, I needed glasses because I was short-sighted. I was sitting down the back, and I didn't have my glasses on, and it looked like they'd pointed to me as a winner. Up I jumped and started moving along my row, sliding past twenty boys into the middle of the hall. People were saying, 'Gower, it's not you.' But by now I was committed — so I just kept going. I remember these All Blacks looking at me like, 'Who's this rooster?' They were a bit bemused and went, 'Oh, here you go, mate, here's a can of Coke.'

The whole school was cracking up. All but the humiliated sports master, who shot daggers at me — it was like I'd shamed the school in front of New Zealand royalty. The laughing went on for ages as I went back to my seat, clutching my can.

At the time, I could never really answer why I'd pulled those crazy stunts. But looking back now, it doesn't take a psychologist to figure out that some of why I was acting up, trying to get a laugh, was a way of offsetting the teasing and bullying. It was a defence. When I made people laugh at my antics, at least they were kind of laughing with me rather than at me.

4.
PISS DRINKING 101

There was a lot of pressure to go to university. My parents had never been, and it was part of their Kiwi dream to get their kids there. It wasn't that classic immigrant story of pushy parents, because I didn't respond very well to being pushed. I was a cruiser. Even though I was brainy, I did the bare minimum through school as a B-and-C-grade student, finishing with what was called a B Bursary, which pretty much meant average.

But throughout my school years, The Olds talked about it all the time. 'Go to university, get more opportunities than we did.' So after all the shit I'd caused at school, it was probably just a relief that I headed off to Victoria University in Wellington. All my older cousins went into the trades and onto a farm, so I was the first of the grandchildren to go to university. I didn't really appreciate what it meant to Mum and Dad.

By this stage, the Old Man had been made redundant from

the power station. He and Mum started a small business; they'd do the accounts around the kitchen table and I'd hear them on the phone when they lost customers and suffered all the stress that goes with making a buck for yourself. They worked hard, and they wanted me to have a better life.

I had no idea what I was going to do. None of my parents' friends had been to university, none of my friends' parents had either. I barely knew any doctors, lawyers or engineers — or journalists, come to think of it. I had some interest in politics. While at school I even went for a day's work experience in Parliament with the New Plymouth Labour MP Harry Duynhoven, who knew my dad.

I was good at arguing, so I thought being a lawyer would be perfect, but I didn't have the grades. You needed an A Bursary to get straight in and I had a B Bursary. So I thought I'd start off doing a Bachelor of Arts, and figure it out from there. The joke at the time was that BA stood for 'Bugger All'. It soon became clear that I would be majoring in the art of piss drinking.

”

I started off in the Victoria House hall of residence, and I quickly met a lot of guys from other parts of New Zealand who were also keen to get good marks in Piss Drinking 101. We were in trouble in the first few days for drinking on the roof of the hostel's third floor, having climbed out a trapdoor to get there.

I actually started studying drinking at high school. The first time I got drunk was when I was fifteen. My Old Lady had gone to Ireland to see her relatives and Dad was in charge for six weeks.

He had a birthday party and bought a keg, and I got pissed and ended up spewing on the front lawn of the neighbours' house. Dad and some of his friends found me and put me to bed. In the morning, Dad said, 'Got a bit drunk last night?' And that was it.

By the sixth form, my mates and I were regularly having parties and drinking at home. The drinking age was twenty, but it was pretty easy to get hold of alcohol ourselves. I can remember buying booze at sixteen, even with my braces and zits. The Olds had an account down at the local wholesalers and I could just walk in, pick up a tray of beer and say 'put it on the account for Gower' — and they would. Mum would see it on the account but rather than hitting the roof, she'd pay it.

Obviously Mum and Dad had a pretty relaxed attitude to booze. But that wasn't peculiar to them — it was part of the culture, the classic Kiwi lifestyle at the time. Their stance was that it was better if we were drinking at home where they could keep an eye on us, with Mum offering us sausage rolls to fill our stomachs.

”

At uni, there was nobody making us sausage rolls. There was no supervision whatsoever. I was a typical student in a massive party scene. I even remember once getting drunk before an exam.

There were brushes with the cops, too, including after I had a play-fight with a mate outside a student bar. As we rolled around wrestling, I ended up putting my hand through the window of a hat shop — I've still got the scar. The cops arrived when I was at the hospital: 'There's been some students seen smashing the window of the hat shop. Was it you?' I was sitting there, pissed, bleeding from my wrist — of course it was me. Busted. Once my wrist was stitched up, the cops arrested me, took me to the cells and charged me with wilful damage. I had to appear in the Wellington District Court the next day.

It was the first time I'd seen a charge sheet or been in a courtroom. As I stood there with my bandaged wrist, the judge didn't even look at me. I'm not even sure he looked up from the paperwork. He gave me diversion, a scheme for first-time offenders where if I admitted what I'd done I wouldn't have a criminal record.

You could call it a lucky break, and it should have been a wake-up call about my drinking — but I was back into it straight away, probably that night. It was a culture of drink, drink, drink. Hard drinking every weekend without fail. Hard drinking some weeknights. Drinking games. Sculling pints, sculling jugs. Drinking a box of 24 beers, then hitting the spirits. Getting out of control at out-of-control flat warmings. Funnels for fun, yard glasses at twenty-firsts, the university Easter tourney that was a gigantic annual piss trip. Piss trips just because we could. The works. You could dress it up as socialising and making friends, but really, drinking was the central force of my life at that time.

”

It wasn't all a write-off. One night on the piss got me some future work experience. I was with two mates carousing down Wellington's Courtenay Place well after midnight; the nightclubs were pumping but we decided to grab a feed. We ducked into a

Chinese takeaway and were waiting for our orders when the door swung open.

It was New Zealand First leader Winston Peters and a couple of his offsiders. It was a sight I would come to know very well in later years. But this was new. We couldn't believe our eyes. Two of us were politics students, so seeing this late-1990s version of Peters — already a powerful figure in New Zealand politics, full of swagger, style and sting — was bloody exciting.

It shouldn't have been that much of a surprise — Peters was known to be out after dark on Courtenay Place quite a lot. As for us? Yeah, it was certainly not our first night out in the capital's notorious drinking zone.

We sat quietly for a moment but as you may have predicted, my smart-arse streak went into overdrive. I couldn't help myself: 'Well, look who's just walked in,' I said. 'Bruce Beetham.'

We'd just been studying Beetham and his Social Credit party, a political entity that had been a third-party battler, yet only ever managed to win two seats during its heights in the 1980s.

Pretending to confuse Peters for Beetham was a real dig — it was a low blow, like if some cheeky prick these days deliberately called me Duncan Garner. My mates cracked up laughing. Peters heard us and came straight over to have a go, unleashing one of his vitriolic and acerbic barrages. We were slanging back at him; it was all go.

I reckon I got the final say, getting in a great one-liner about how he lost in the Winebox, and now he'd lost in the takeaway. We rushed out onto the street, laughing — holy shit! A couple of young politics students, and we'd just had a row with Winston Peters!

I've never told Peters this, not even when we shared nights out together on Courtenay Place later in our careers. If he does remember, I'm sure he would have a different version to tell.

"

Away from the nightlife, I was battling through my degree with average grades. But I was a good reader and I got into the American beat-generation writers like Allen Ginsberg, who wrote the incredible poem 'Howl', a crazy outcry at society, and Jack Kerouac, who wrote *On The Road* about a drug-fuelled trip across the United States. I wasn't into the literature so much, it was more like, *Fuck, these guys are cool.*

I was also studying history, in classes taught by James Belich, known for his research on the New Zealand Wars. He started talking about the Taranaki Wars of the 1860s, and a name I'd never heard before — Riwha Tītokowaru. Even though a lot of what Belich was telling us about had happened just down the road from where I'd grown up, or just around the coast, I'd had no idea. I was hooked.

Tītokowaru led his people in a campaign against the confiscation of land, presiding over several victories that struck at the heart of the fledgling colony. Belich argued that Tītokowaru may have been the best military leader Aotearoa ever produced. He used his strategic genius and resilience to outwit and outfox opponents, including the notorious Prussian soldier who joined the colonial forces, Gustavus von Tempsky, who was killed in an attack on a Tītokowaru stronghold in 1868. I read more about this rangatira, learning that, later in life, he'd turned from being a warrior to a pacifist, urging reconciliation and peace. He'd been able to change his ways, his desires and his methods.

So much of his story spoke to me, then and now. Again, it was, *Fuck, this guy is cool.*

There's a famous whakatauākī or proverb attributed to Tītokowaru: 'E kore ahau e mate, kāore ahau e mate. Ka mate anō te mate, ka ora anō ahau.' ('I shall not die, I shall not die. When death itself is dead, I shall be alive.') His words resonated with me, and matched what I knew about the character of the people of Taranaki — strong, resilient, courageous outsiders. But Tītokowaru's story was new to me. *Why didn't I know any of this?*

It didn't feel right that there could be these remarkable stories of courage and leadership, and no one knew about them. I remember telling my mates about Tītokowaru; they were like 'Whoa!', and it felt good to tell the yarn. I didn't know it at the time, but I'd finally found something that inspired me — telling stories.

”

Growing up, news was always around, spread out like a feast each morning. We had the *Taranaki Daily News* delivered and it would be there on the breakfast bar each day. I'd hop up on the stool and devour its pages while I crunched on Molenberg toast with peanut butter, jam and cinnamon. Mum was always there, efficiently and diligently making our lunches.

My first role in the news business was as a paperboy, cruising around on my bike to deliver New Plymouth's midweek paper after school. Sometimes I got to deliver the *Taranaki Daily News* when my mate was away, but getting your hands on one of those rounds was tough because they'd be passed from brother to brother. It was like a *Succession*-style media cartel you couldn't break into unless you were in 'the family'.

My first memory of really liking the news was in 1989 when I'd religiously read the sports section, especially during the All Blacks' tour of Wales and Ireland. At university, the *Dominion* and the *Evening Post* were delivered to the common room at my hostel. At the time, the Gene and Eugene Thomas murder trial was on, a sensational case where the father and son insurance and investment brokers were shot dead in their Wellington office. An antiques dealer and gun enthusiast, John Barlow, was eventually convicted of their murders but only after three controversial trials. I'd gorge on every word about the case.

When I went flatting in my second year at Vic, even though I was a poor student spending most of my spare money on drinking, I got a subscription to the *Dominion*, which was a bit unusual. One of my flatmate's parents was really impressed I did that, not realising any good influence ended there.

'Oh, look — they're getting the *Dom* in the flat each day, thanks to Paddy.' What they didn't realise was I also owned the flat's beer bong.

"

Around this time, I was quietly discovering some journalistic heroes. During the university holidays, I went to the New Plymouth library and read the *New Zealand Herald* for its political writers, particularly John Armstrong, the political editor. By the end of my degree, journalism had become a thing I wanted to do. But the journalism schools all wanted people who had some work experience and I hadn't written a thing. I was twenty years old and had a BA in Politics. I was in no way ready for a job. So it was back to uni for an honours year in politics. This was really freaking my parents out; I was suddenly looking like a permanent student, studying stuff that wasn't leading anywhere.

I did have a plan, though. I'd knock off the honours and write stories for *Salient*, the Vic student magazine, so that I had some clippings — stories that I could then use to prove my interest in writing to the journalism schools.

For my honours, I chose to do a media in politics paper involving research on media reporting of defence policy. I started studying with Professor Margaret Clark, and she asked a retired politics professor, Les Cleveland, to help because he'd been a journalist, photographer and former soldier.

We'd talk about how the media reported on defence, the gist of which was that it was a really important topic but it didn't get a fair go. When I finished my paper, Margaret sent a copy to Les, who replied with a hilarious letter. 'Thanks for the Gower opus,' he wrote. 'Turned out alright.'

He wrote that he hoped I'd get into journalism school, but if I didn't, he had an alternative. 'It occurs to me that, as it happens, he would also make suitable material for the army. I know the army is a rather downtrodden institution at the moment, but nevertheless it is a substantial profession. They're always looking for good graduate talent to commission. If you happen to be chatting to him sometime perhaps you could delicately mention the possibility.'

Margaret never did mention the possibility, delicately or otherwise — I only learnt of it when she gave me the letter later on. But I can tell you right now that I was most certainly not suitable material for the army. A classic letter, though, from a guy who had watched me closely for a year and thought I'd be a fair sort of journalist and, if not, good for the army.

”

I started writing for *Salient* as planned: I had a regular sports column called 'It's a Funny Old Game', and I'd write the odd article, too. My first was about a psychology lecturer who'd written a research paper on the inflammatory language used during media coverage of the 1997 scandal around New Zealand First MP Tuku Morgan. He'd been involved in the establishment of a Māori-language broadcaster and it emerged that during that time he'd spent $89 of public money on a pair of Hugo Boss underpants.

The *Salient* piece was headlined 'Skin Deep — the polarisation of New Zealand media', and it basically said the Morgan controversy was a media beat-up and that the *Dominion* in particular had used racist, over-the-top language. We got into a bit of shit because I didn't contact the *Dominion* for comment — my first complaint. It's interesting to read the story nowadays, given some of the shenanigans I got up to later in my media life. Put it this way: I started on a very high horse.

My research paper must have been okay as I earned first-class honours. My parents were pleased I finally seemed to be on track, as journalism was an actual job as opposed to 'political science'.

They were a bit anxious, though, about the fact I was going to have to do another year at university — I'd already been studying for four years. This was in the days of student loans up the wazoo, with interest and none of this fees-free business.

I'd decided I wanted to go to AUT in Auckland for a postgraduate diploma in journalism. I liked the look of their brochure, but I was also keen to get away from Welly. And I'd somehow figured out that most of the jobs were in Auckland, so it would be good to get closer to the industry. My application with the *Salient* clippings went in and . . . I got rejected. I didn't make it. What was I going to do?

One of my other professors was political scientist Stephen Levine, and I spoke to him about my issue. The head of the AUT course at the time was Ruth Thomas. Stephen reassuringly told me, 'Oh, I know Ruth.' He was Jewish and Ruth was Jewish. He wrote Ruth a letter saying he had a student who had been rejected from the course but that I was very keen on the media and I was a good person. Next minute, after someone pulled out of the course, I was accepted.

Going up to Auckland was the fresh start I needed. I also felt like I'd found my tribe. There were about 25 people on the course, who all really wanted to be journos, mostly recent graduates but some with a bit of life experience, and plenty of characters.

It was all go, very focused, a gear shift for me. Even just being in the class newsroom was exhilarating. As much as it was a fresh start, though, some things didn't really change. At lunchtime on the first day, me and another guy went and had a beer. And of course at the end of the day we all went for drinks. Stress release, you know?

We got a lot of practice finding and writing stories under supervision and getting them published — it was a thrill, no matter the topic. Whether it was about toilet blocks, community opposition to car parking, a kid who won a recipe competition — I was writing actual stories. During an internship at the *Waikato Times*, I was assigned a feature — a feature! — on something called Tae Bo, a late-'90s kickboxing fitness fad that was never heard of again.

Towards the end of the year, I went to the *New Zealand Herald* for another internship and it went well.

On the last day, the chief reporter, Shenagh Gleeson, pulled me aside. She said there were some jobs for junior reporters coming up and that I should apply. I was in no way a shoo-in and I was desperate to get a job, so to cover my bases, I sent letters to every daily newspaper in the country asking if they had any vacancies.

By that stage, I'd finished my diploma, so I went home to New Plymouth and waited. Then the replies started rolling in. One after another, a paper trail of rejection from the *Northern Advocate* to the *Southland Times*. The editor of *The Press*, Tim Pankhurst, not only said there wasn't a job, but also pointed out I had an apostrophe in the wrong place in my application letter. Nice touch.

Still I waited for the *Herald*.

Mum and Dad must have been losing hope — had that five years of study been for nothing? Dad couldn't believe that at age 22, I still didn't have a job. I'd taken to sleeping in quite a bit, and signed up for the dole. One morning, I heard the phone ring and Dad answering it. Next thing I heard footsteps coming. 'It's for you.' It was Wayne Harman, editorial manager of the *Herald*. 'Hello, Patrick,' he said. 'Look, we'd like to offer you—'

'Yes. Yes, I'll take it!' I didn't even wait to hear what the job was.

'Hang on, hang on . . .' he said.

But I was too excited, so I didn't take in any of the details: that I was going to be working a night shift, starting at 6 p.m., a role no one had done on a permanent basis in the *Herald*'s 137-year history. A seven-and-a-half hour stretch, no dinner break, Sunday to Friday. Night duty.

Honestly, even if I had heard properly, I wouldn't have cared. It was a job at a newsroom I'd fallen in love with. Dad said 'You fucking beauty', and we danced around. Mum was out for a walk with a friend so I went and stood on the deck, waiting for her to get back. I was so eager to tell her.

I heard the gate squeak, and I called out as soon as I saw her coming around the corner. 'Mum, I got the job at the *Herald*!'

She squealed. I'd never heard her squeal before. But she squealed with happiness, barrelled up the stairs and launched herself at me. She gave me this big hug, squeezing me tight against her. I just remember standing on that deck, my mum hugging me, Taranaki's warm summer sun shining down on us. I'd made Mum proud, really proud.

Mum and Dad's dreams had come true; their son had a good job. My dreams, well, they were just beginning.

5.
THE NIGHT TRAIN

Newsrooms are amazing places when you first walk into them. Certainly the newsrooms of 25 years ago, anyway. There's nothing quite like them. Though there were desks and padded chairs on wheels, they weren't offices. Too shambolic and cluttered. Though they were full of knowledge and shelves of reference books, they definitely weren't libraries. Too noisy and chaotic. (And there was lots of swearing!) Though there were wide, open-plan floors and frequent bursts of shouting, they weren't stock-exchange trading rooms. There was no money, even then.

When I arrived from New Plymouth in February 2000 as its first-ever full-time night-duty reporter, the *Herald* newsroom was brimming with characters. Even the paper itself had a nickname, 'Granny *Herald*', because it had been a bit of a nana at times.

The building was right in the centre of Auckland, on the corner of Albert and Wyndham streets, and had been there since the newspaper was first published in 1863. It was a relic of the times when the printing was done on-site. There was a car park called the 'cart dock', from the days when horses and carts would come in to get the papers. One of the rickety-rackety old lifts with a cage door took you to two basements where once upon a time the presses had noisily squeezed out the news. By 2000, the machines had long since gone out to Ellerslie, leaving ghostly, cavernous, abandoned spaces.

Upstairs, on the third floor, the daily miracle of news still played out. In the corner of the newsroom, a police scanner blared out the radio traffic of fire, police and ambulance, a jumble of crackles and coded messages. 'K-99' was a well-ablaze fire. Reporters half-listened to hear if there were any buildings burning down or cop chases.

There were reporters who focused on council news and there were court reporters. There were photographers with eagle eyes, colourful language and an over-abundance of adrenaline. In the corner, there was a long-haired young fella 'uploading' stories to something called 'the internet' — no one was sure if that was going to work out. Sitting alongside a vast window that promised great views but only overlooked the cart dock, there was a bank of sub-editors who sharpened our sentences and mended our grammar. Tucked around the corners were the specialists — business reporters, sports reporters and feature writers.

And then there was Tony Wall, who everyone called 'Wallo'. He was the alpha male of the newsroom, one of the police reporters — so-called because he covered crimes and emergencies. Anyone who knows Wallo will think that what I'm about to say is crazy talk, because not a lot of people think Wallo is cool. But

I'm genuine: I thought he was the coolest person I'd ever seen in my life. He had a shaved head and wore a leather jacket, jeans and no tie. The newsroom trend of the day for guys was pastel-coloured shirts, ties and dress pants. Everyone wore the same thing. Not Wallo. He stood alone. I even admired the way he carried his notebook, folded up and tucked in his hand like a fashion accessory rather than a piece of stationery.

My desk was right next to his. I couldn't believe my luck. He immediately started passing on nuggets of information and story ideas. I loved his stories — big crime cases and scoops about dodgy deeds — and I dreamt of doing them myself someday. I wanted to be just like him.

”

It wasn't long before Wallo gave me the nickname 'Night Train'. It seemed appropriate — I'd steam in each night, 6 p.m., right on time. The other reporters quickly started calling me it, too. I really liked it; Night Train was an awesome nickname.

Each shift, I'd head up in the lift and start walking to my desk, but often the bosses would intercept me to give me an assignment, something they desperately needed done. Each night was a thrill. You just never knew what was going to come your way.

In my first week, one of the old-timers who'd been around for decades, Arnold Pickmere, said he'd noticed a ruckus at a building site in Remuera on his way to work. I was sent out to see if it was a story. Being rich, old Remmers, there were some nosy neighbours next door, and I was invited into this very flash house, and through to a living room stuffed with antiques and plush furniture — and a vast window that overlooked the harbour and also helpfully gave a perfect view down into the building site.

I got a blow-by-blow eyewitness account of how a bunch of plasterers had been taken away when police and other official-looking types swarmed the place. I went back to the newsroom and hit the phones, calling one person who'd put me onto another person, and eventually confirmed the workers were illegal immigrants. This was a bit of an issue in Auckland at the time, and suddenly one of the paper's most senior reporters, Naomi Larkin, was helping me and we were even chasing the Minister of Immigration for comment as we rushed to deadline. The next morning, I woke up at a mate's place where I'd been crashing while I tried to find a flat, and I got him to drive me to the dairy. 'I reckon I might have my first front-page lead, bro.' That was the most coveted spot in the paper for a news reporter. When I walked out, my mate could tell by my big grin — yep, sure enough. I was on the front page. Seeing my name there was just surreal. I was stoked.

I couldn't believe that from this tip from keen-eyed, gentlemanly Arnold, we'd been able to turn it into the most important story in the paper the next day. Arnold came over to shake my hand and said, 'Good on you.' The Night Train was underway.

”

Most nights, my target was the lead brief — one or two sentences at the top of page three. It was usually something that happened late that I'd chase down for the news editors to whip into the paper at the last minute, like a fire out in Glen Innes or a flash flood down in Maramarua.

Those titbits usually came from my bread and butter work, which was phoning emergency control rooms around the country — fire, police and ambulance — and asking them if anything was happening. Most times it was a mundane routine. 'Hello, Inspector. It's Patrick Gower from the *Herald* here. Anything happening?'

'No.'

'Thank you.' Repeat every two hours.

Because I'd do it so often, I'd get to know some of these cops and build up a bit of a rapport, so sometimes you might get a clue. 'Well, actually, Patrick, there's something brewing in Northland we're keeping an eye on — give me a ring back in fifteen minutes.' Bang. You were away. Could be a robbery, could be a cat stuck up a tree, you just didn't know, but you'd be ringing back on the dot, fifteen minutes later, to find out if you had your prized page-three brief. It might even be enough for a story itself, which I soon started referring to as 'yarns'.

At the same time I was getting an education in journalism each night, learning how to hone the craft. Another reporter I sat near was Bernard Orsman, who was the Auckland Council reporter. He had a dog-eared contact book bulging with people's home and mobile numbers.

I'd hear Bernard working the phones and getting the inside oil on the council. He had amazing sources.

This was when there was still a tree on One Tree Hill, and one night, Bernard broke the story that the tree was going to be taken down by the council. It had been damaged in two chainsaw protests in 1994 and 1999, and was now quite sick and dying. Behind closed doors, the council decided to remove it, but they wanted to keep it quiet. They were trying to bring the tree down without anyone knowing. Bernard broke the yarn and it was huge.

The next night, I was sent to One Tree Hill to see if anyone was up there.

'You never know, you might find someone and get a couple of quotes,' the boss said. You've got to remember this was before the days of social media, so we had no idea what was going on. It wasn't like there were people posting to Instagram.

Off I went with a photographer, having signed out a gigantic brick of a cell phone, an old-school Nokia. And bugger me days, there were heaps of people there, lining the road to the top. People who had read Bernard's story and had come to say goodbye to the tree. An impromptu vigil.

I got out my notebook and started interviewing people. There was a guy with a guitar playing the U2 song 'One Tree Hill'. One regular Kiwi dad was there and he said his sons were away on their OE; he wanted to be there, not just for himself but for them, because they'd lived and played under One Tree Hill, and as he spoke he got emotional. I carried on marching up the hill, scribbling down as many quotes as I could from as many people as I could. It was close to deadline when I got to the top, so I pulled out the brick and punched in the newsroom number and told the boss there were hundreds of people, from the bottom of the hill to the top.

He asked, 'Have you spoken to any of them?'

I replied, 'Yep, I've got quotes, names — the lot.'

Then he just said, 'Get back as soon as you can.' And hung up. Urgency trumped niceties.

We raced across the city, back to the office. There wasn't even time for me to type up my story; I had to read out the quotes to the boss who typed them straight into the text. They changed the front page, adding my quotes to Bernard's follow-up story, and used this amazing photo of the tree at night. The next morning it was the front-page 'splash', which meant it was splashed all over it.

It was the first time I knew I'd been part of history. That was the end of the tree on One Tree Hill and I'd been there, helping to record this moment, adding people's voices and emotions. Until then I'd just been bashing out yarns, which I was loving. But I knew this was different. I've been privileged enough to experience it quite a few times since. You can detect when there's something really big going down; it's like there's something in the air. They call it the weight of history for a reason, because it feels heavy.

As a cub reporter, I'd also seen how Bernard had broken a story using hardcore journalism and revealed a truth to the city, exposed solid facts — and given people a chance to say goodbye to the tree that meant so much to them. I'd seen these people myself, like that dad saying goodbye for his sons. That night on One Tree Hill changed everything for me. This wasn't just a job. Going out and getting stories and telling people about them was much more than that. I'd discovered my calling in life.

”

On weeks like that, the thrill was immense. I'd finish my working week on Friday at 1.30 a.m., but I'd sleep then come back in on Friday nights to meet with the crew at the pub across the road from the *Herald*, The Shakespeare. I really liked letting off steam with Wallo and the other reporters, and telling yarns about the yarns we'd been telling.

One of the first nights I went along, there was a queue at the bar when I arrived. I was talking with this friendly guy who was a partner of a workmate, a really lovely couple. When he got to the front of the queue, he ordered two beers for himself and whatever his partner was drinking. I asked him why the two beers and he said, 'I hate queueing for my next beer so I always just get two.' I thought, *Eureka! This guy is a genius!* And from then on, whenever I arrived at the bar I'd buy two beers straight away, no matter what. The first one to take the edge off, and then you could just relax straight into your second without having to queue up again. It was a habit I kept for the next two decades, 'double-fisting'.

I thought I'd had an education in drinking at university, but there were a few lessons still to learn in those early years of journalism. One of them was at the journalism awards, which was really just a massive annual piss-up for the industry. I was a finalist in the student journalist category for my stories the year before, including that feature I'd written on Tae Bo down in the Waikato. Cruising along with the other reporters to what I thought was a swanky gig was enough for me, but next minute my name was called out.

Legendary media personalities Bill Ralston and Janet Wilson were the MCs and I had another moment reminiscent of the episode with the All Blacks and the can of Coke at high school. I caused a ripple of mirth among all the journos when I headed up to collect my prize — I didn't know which way to go, staggered around, and went up the wrong side of the stage. I remember Ralston cracking up, and then I got even more confused and stalked across the stage the wrong way again to get off. All the journos were laughing and wondering, *Who the hell is this guy?*

We all went to The Shakespeare for the after-party and I had my official induction into real journalistic drinking. It was wild: a bar table got smashed to smithereens for no reason whatsoever; during a rolling, drunken wrestle, a mad-dog photographer pinched my left nipple with his knuckles so hard it was bruised and swollen for days; and I got so blotto, I lost my $500 winner's cheque. I guess I'd earned my patch in the drinking side of journalism.

”

After a year as the Night Train, my boss called me and told me I was being dispatched to the Hamilton branch office. I remember thinking, *This is an interesting 'promotion'.* But it was an order rather than a request, and at least I would be awake in the daytime. Since the *Herald* was an Auckland-based paper, it was like being in a satellite away from the mothership. As words of encouragement, another one of the bosses told me to view it like I was a foreign correspondent. Except I was in Hamilton, so that felt hard to pull off. One of my first stories was about a university men's volleyball team getting into trouble for being sponsored by an escort agency and wearing T-shirts with the slogan 'Get Shagged in Horny Hamilton'.

Away from the relentless ambulance-chasing as the Night Train, being in Hamilton meant I had time to get into some of the bigger, gruntier stories — covering murder trials and being in the room when a jury came back with its verdict had that vibe of witnessing something heavy going down.

The biggest thing that happened while I was in Hamilton was when the *Herald* became a story itself. Journalists in the union went on strike in a classic dispute that only unionised journos could have over a complicated point of principle that I have long forgotten. It was really awkward as most of the senior journos were on strike but the bosses were still working and I felt really torn, especially as I was just starting out. I wanted to stand with the crew, but I wanted to be a good employee, too. It was a bloody awful feeling. I just loved breaking yarns and suddenly we couldn't.

Things got increasingly divided, there was all this talk of scabs and picket lines, and I realised that I was someone who liked everyone to be together. The bosses were struggling to put the paper out; one day they had to run a big photo of ducklings crossing a road to fill up a page, so it seemed like the strike was working. Then I was in bed one morning and Dad rang to say turn on the TV — the 9/11 terror attacks were on.

This meant the bosses had international stories for weeks to come so there'd be no need for duckling yarns. It was the biggest story in the world and I wasn't part of it, and my rivals at the *Waikato Times* ran an amazing yarn about a Hamiltonian who was in New York ordering a hot dog when the planes hit. I was absolutely gutted when I saw it; I wished I was doing yarns like that, and I actually cried my eyes out in disappointment. The strike was soon broken, but it was still a bloody long strike at nineteen days.

It always made me smile years later when I was covering the Labour Party's troubles and lots of unionists and MPs would go after me, and it felt like I was public enemy number one for the lefties. I'd quietly laugh to myself, *I've actually done more time on strike than all of you put together.*

"

I was eventually called back to the mothership in Auckland and my dream job of the time — on the police desk where my old idol Wallo used to work (he was now a sharpshooter in the investigative unit). Auckland was going through many changes — gang crime, ethnic violence and drug use were on the rise — and I was reporting from the frontlines of it all.

One of the biggest stories was the December 2001 triple murder at the Panmure RSA by William Dwane Bell. It was the worst murder in Auckland for a long time, off the scale in terms of violence. During the depositions hearing — the part of the proceedings where the Crown has to produce evidence to convince a judge there is enough to go to trial — I managed to get a scoop over all the other media. However, the truth was I only got the story because I was pathetic at shorthand.

At journalism school, learning shorthand was one of the key requirements to passing. I was utterly useless at it. We had to get 80 words per minute, and every time someone passed they'd leave the shorthand class, quite smugly, knowing they'd get their diploma. I was toiling away at the end with two other shorthand battlers, and one day all three of us were certain we'd failed yet another test. The teacher took in our tests and said, 'Congratulations, you've passed.' We looked at her, wondering *What the?*, got the old nod-and-a-wink, as they say, then exchanged knowing smiles and said no more as she waved us on our happy way.

I never used shorthand once I started working, and that made court reporting a bit tricky. But at deposition hearings in those days, after a witness gave evidence, the court staff read back what had been said so the witness could check that it was an accurate account. This was fantastic for me, as I'd get a second chance to note stuff down.

On the first day of Bell's depositions, the star witness, a guy who'd been involved but had dramatically turned to give evidence against Bell, finished his testimony late in the day and the court staff began to read back his evidence. All the other journalists on the packed press bench left to meet their deadlines. Not me — I needed to check what had been said since my notes were so bad.

While this very laborious process was going on, Bell leapt out of the dock where he was sitting and lunged towards the witness — a psychopath was on the loose in the courtroom. It was chaos. The prosecutor dived under the desk, and I was calculating if I could jump out the window. Everyone's instinct was to get the hell out of the way — except the cop in charge of the investigation, Detective Inspector Gavin Jones. His instinct was to protect, so he sprung forward and wedged himself between Bell and the witness, which showed incredible guts.

In the aftermath, as everyone started breathing normally again, I realised old muggins no-shorthand PG was the only journalist who had the yarn. I couldn't believe my luck.

I took off, down the courthouse escalator — I'm not even sure my feet touched the steps — sprinted across the road to the *Herald*, straight past the lift, strode up the stairs two at a time, traversed the newsroom like a gazelle, and made a beeline directly towards the editor for the first time in my career. I blurted out, 'Bell has just attacked a witness and no other media were there!' Of course, I didn't mention why they weren't. It was the front-page lead the next morning, and the reporters who'd missed the story would have had some explaining to do.

Bell was eventually convicted of the murders, and on the day he was found guilty I had a package of stories ready to go. Every spare moment I had, I'd been going out to South Auckland to track down people who knew him, or knew about what had happened, to piece together what was behind these horrific murders.

One of the stories that one of Bell's mates told me was that Bell had used a pure form of methamphetamine called 'P'. This was one of the first big yarns on P. It wasn't really on the radar back then, and hadn't even been mentioned in the trial, but we were starting to join the dots about the rise in hyper-violent crimes. Back then, I only saw it as a crime story. But as my career went on, I'd come to have a different opinion altogether.

6. PATRICK GOWER: ON PROZAC

While I was cracking yarns at the *Herald*, my mates were in London calling up from various nightclubs and pubs to bang away at me with various versions of 'get your arse over here, PG'. So after a few years, it was time to head off on the OE. It wasn't so much about getting overseas journalism experience, but rather overseas partying experience.

I did manage to land a job with Jane's, an old-school English publisher with a military focus, on a magazine called *Police Review*, writing about the 43 police forces of the UK. Later I shifted to *TNT Magazine* — remember, this was before Facebook — which was a way for Kiwis, Aussies and South Africans to connect and keep up with news from home and the expat community. In reality, though, journalism was on hold — this was an extended piss trip.

I also managed to connect with relatives, including going to

Galway and Donegal in Ireland where Mum's family came from. My nana grew up in Gweedore, a town on the wild Atlantic coast in the north-west of Ireland, on the border with Northern Ireland. The town is known as a stronghold of the Irish language, with one of the highest percentages of Irish-speaking people in the country.

Some of my relatives ran what was known as a Gaeltacht experience, a full-immersion language centre for school students where they could go on courses to learn to speak Gaelic. I stayed with them for the New Year break, sleeping in one of the bunkrooms when — luckily, as it turned out — there were no students around.

It was a brilliant, if wild, time hanging out with my Donegal cuzzies, hearing them speak Gaelic, and getting to know them better. One of my relatives, Pearse Doherty, was a political candidate for Sinn Féin, the movement previously linked to the Irish Republican Army. I went along to one of his fundraisers, a fun gambling night. Pearse is in the Irish Parliament now.

On New Year's Eve itself, my cousins took me out drinking. Their style was different to ours but no less potent. We didn't have our first drink until about 10 p.m., which seemed weird, but when we started they put the hammer down and went hard. We drank a lot of Guinness, obviously, and we drank it fast. The gin and tonics started coming in quickly between the Guinnesses, and I eventually had to start hiffing booze into pot plants because of the amount they were plying me with. We stumbled around cosy pubs where musicians performed in the corners, including some fiddle-playing relatives of the famous singer Enya (who actually does come from Gweedore) — or at least they said they were.

After a massive session we went into the town's takeaway, run by another cousin, and ordered the local delicacy: 'curry chips', hot chips smothered in curry sauce. After that it was back to the bunkroom, though, in all honesty, I don't remember that. Much of the evening was a blackout.

I woke up to that horrible feeling of *Did I power-chuck?* Which was followed by that even more horrible feeling of opening my eyes and seeing that, yes, indeed I had power-chucked. I had sprayed the walls with this Guinness-tinged, orangey-yellow, curry-smelling gunge. It was everywhere. After initially checking out the sheer scale of the spray and thinking *Holy shit — how am I even capable of this?*, my next thought was quickly *How the hell am I going to clean this up?*

Bear in mind that, although these were my relatives, I didn't know my hosts that well. What ensued was something like the scene out of *Trainspotting* where Spud desperately tries to clean up after a very messy night. I used the sheets to wipe up the room as best I could, then made a dash for the washing machine and had a wrestle with one of my cousins who was offering to take the bedding off me. 'No, no, no — I've got it,' I said, desperately trying to cover up what I'd done to the place. As if she didn't know; the place almost needed to be sanded and painted to truly hide my curry-Guinness spray job.

”

I was over London life but wasn't quite ready to come home. I had a mate living in Canada so I headed to Vancouver for a fresh start. After sorting out visas and making contact with the *Vancouver*

Sun, I arrived, but I'd only been there a couple of days when a phone call changed everything. It was The Olds. They were pretty quiet and weird. Dad said: 'Your mum's got something to tell you.'

Mum said nothing, there was just silence. Then Dad said: 'Your mother's got cancer. It's lung cancer.'

As soon as I hung up, I googled lung cancer and read that it was virtually unsurvivable — remember, this was eighteen years ago, before many of the new next-generation drugs. I knew I had to make a decision quickly but I didn't know who to talk to about it. Normally you'd ask your parents for advice, but they had enough to deal with. My nana was still alive but she was in a rest-home hospital and not well. I rang my mum's sister, but she was in shock. Her only advice was that this was a decision I had to make for myself. All of a sudden I realised that this was what being an adult was about. At 29, I'd had a golden run. Here was reality smacking me in the face.

I made the only decision I could: to get back to New Zealand ASAP. I arrived in New Plymouth after about two-and-a-half years away and my mum and dad weren't there to greet me. Mum couldn't face meeting me so publicly at the airport, so they'd asked a family friend to collect me. We pulled up outside my family home. Suddenly, there I was, at one o'clock on a weekday afternoon in Taranaki, yanked out of a life I was just starting on the other side of the world.

Mum was in the front garden, pulling out weeds. I looked at her and, physically, she didn't seem any different. Then she turned to face me, and I immediately saw a look in her eyes I'd never seen before. She didn't look frightened. She didn't even look happy to see me. She looked ashamed. I know it's really sad to say that. But she looked ashamed of herself, and embarrassed. And I knew why.

She had lung cancer after being a smoker her whole life. I'd asked her to give up when I was younger, and now here we were. Maybe she thought I was going to be angry with her? Of course I wasn't. Besides, there was no time for that.

I felt awkward: who wants to see their parents like that? No one wants to see their parents ashamed. I wasn't ashamed of her, I wasn't embarrassed and I wasn't angry. As the saying goes, what's done is done. So I just told her what I did feel: 'I love you, Mum.'

We went inside and walked into the living room and sat on the couch, as the Taranaki winter sun shone through the window. I lay down and put my head in her lap, like I used to when I was a kid, like I had on that drive from Rotorua when I'd smashed my teeth.

She stroked my hair, and I felt her take the power back. Her instinct was to comfort me, to use that innate connection between a mother and a child to assure them that everything would be fine. Of course it wasn't. Absolutely it wasn't.

But her fingers brushed my hair and she gently said: 'I'm so proud of you. It's going to be okay.' I can still feel her hand on my head, and the warm sun on us, the light in the room. It was a final moment of innocence.

”

The world spun faster and faster out of control. One of my Old Man's best friends, Keith, had died of cancer, so Dad and I went to the funeral only days after I got back; father and son together, mourning his mate. I remember during the speeches I was reeling at Mum's diagnosis. I remember watching his family and just thinking: *Holy fuck.* I had my eyes on Keith's son, James, who I used to play with as a kid at barbecues, running around in our backyards. Now he was in the Army, and he was standing there at the front, straight upright, taking on the mantle of leadership within his family. It brought home to me what I was about to have to go through, too. I wasn't ready. I had no life skills to deal with any of this, no ability to take in what the fuck was going on.

Within a fortnight, Nana died, and next thing we were up at her funeral in Auckland, Mum puffed up on steroids burying her own mother as she tried to stare down death herself; the family all crammed together in one of those tiny funeral homes. I know I must have been cooked because when it came time to say a few words I didn't say anything. It was grim. It was heavy. And I had no way of stopping it.

We were on the path that's familiar to so many New Zealand families who've dealt with a loved one with a terminal cancer diagnosis — a long, downward spiral of bad news after bad news after bad news.

”

I'd come back from overseas without a dollar to my name, so thankfully Granny *Herald* took me back in. But that was pretty bleak, too. A lot of characters still dressed in the same clothes as they had when I left. My life was split in two as well. I'd moved back to Auckland for work, but I'd return to New Plymouth every chance I could to help look after Mum.

I was living in a flat in Herne Bay, one of Auckland's swankiest suburbs, but it was in shade all day long. I guess that's the reason it was cheap enough for me to live there. It had a balcony, but during the peak of the day the sun would only tiptoe along the edge, daubing its golden warmth on no more than a metre of the wooden decking. I used to stare out the window and think, *I wish I lived somewhere sunny.* Some days, I wouldn't even go outside. I'd sit all day in the gloom. I'd think about going for a run or walk, but my motivation had vanished. One day when I did go for a run, I struggled to even get around the block.

I got an ear infection and headed to a GP one day. During the consultation, we talked about Mum and I told her about my lethargy. She asked me: 'Do you think you're depressed?' I'd never thought about it. The GP pulled out a brochure and started going through a questionnaire with me. As she put the different symptoms to me, I realised, 'Yep, that's me — tick. Yes, tick. Yes, yes, yes — tick, tick, tick.' At the end, the doctor said, 'Everything tells me you're depressed.'

It sunk in: I was staring at the shade. I couldn't manage to walk outside. 'You could take Prozac,' she said. 'It helps some people in your position function better.' Was this really happening? I was 29 years old, supposedly in the prime of my life. Then I thought, *Well, she's a doctor. She knows what she's talking about. Let's give it a go.* And that was that. I was diagnosed with depression, and prescribed Prozac. I didn't tell anyone.

”

Just a few days after starting the pills, I felt much better. I wasn't as worried about the shade and I had at least some spring in my step. But none of that took away what was going on with Mum. The toll of watching her move closer to the end was excruciating. Back and forth I'd go — Auckland for work, New Plymouth to watch the grim march of cancer's advance.

There were so many things I couldn't get my head around — like how every time I saw her, it was as if she'd been deprived of even more dignity; how going to the pharmacy to collect her pills meant driving home with the front passenger seat piled high with paper bags full of rattling plastic bottles. How could one person swallow so many pills?

And weirdly, Mum had given up smoking. When she was diagnosed, she stopped. For years, we'd encouraged her to quit. And she'd tried different things, even hypnosis. None of it had worked. I'd even used guerilla tactics as a kid, hiding her cigarettes. She got angry about that — they were expensive, even back then — so I changed tack and hid her matches. Mum got around that challenge by lighting her smokes from the gas element in the kitchen. Nothing could stop her. She was addicted.

And yet, here she was, on death's door, finally a non-smoker. It was so illogical — when you have terminal lung cancer, it doesn't matter anymore. Giving up smoking like that would have been massively difficult; Mum would have felt really ratty. But it was this weird gift she gave us because it would have been so hard to see her puffing on cigarettes, knowing what they had done to her.

”

When I was at work in Auckland, I'd try my best to focus on the job, and I did manage to crack a few banger yarns. One of them was one of the best stories I'd ever done. I was working on investigations, mostly for the *Herald*'s Saturday paper, which always looked to land big, agenda-setting scoops. A tip came in about Wither Hills, a wine producer entering awards with a wine that was different to what they were selling on the shelves, when they were supposed to be the same. Punters would buy sauvignon blanc with an award on the label, but it was not the same as the wine the judges had tasted.

I met with wine critic Michael Cooper, one of the greatest wine minds in the country, and he was ready to blow the whistle, with a pile of documents and evidence. He started talking about this sauvignon blanc but I jumped in with a crucial question: 'Back up the truck a second . . . What's a sauvignon blanc?' I knew it was a wine, and that was about it. I didn't know if it was red or white, dry or sweet. Michael looked horrified, and I could see his mind whirring: *Here's the journalist I'm trusting with this huge story and he doesn't know what a sav is?* To Michael's credit, he didn't stop the conversation right there and then. He calmly explained and carried on. After a whole lot more work, and careful explanation of wine matters, I broke the story and ended up winning an award for it — best business story at the 2007 Qantas Media Awards.

I was home in New Plymouth before heading to the ceremony in Wellington. I went into Mum's room to show her the black tuxedo I'd hired for the night and she said to me, 'Chocolate brown.' By that stage, she'd just say random things like that. The cancer had spread to her brain.

By May 2007, Mum was on her way out. The hospice nurses were coming each day to see her at home. Everyone in the family was around, waiting, waiting. The hospice nurse turned up one day and I took a wee break for a walk, and had made it to New Plymouth's famous wind wand, about 1.5 kilometres from home, when my phone rang. I didn't even need to answer to know what it was about. 'Come home.' It was my aunty. I ran as fast as I could, desperate to make it. Desperate to see Mum one last time. I caught my breath as I walked in the door, down the hall, and into the bedroom. There with us all, she drew her last.

I can remember my first thought very clearly: *Thank fuck for that.* I was just so relieved she didn't have to suffer anymore. Her last weeks had been torturous. Slow. Painful.

On the day of the funeral, I doubled the dose of my Prozac — it's not advised, so do not try this at home. Straight after the service, I ducked into Peggy Gordon's, the Irish pub behind St Joseph's Church, and had a Guinness with my schoolmates. Then it was back home for a massive wake, in the best Irish tradition. I conked out in the lounge from a combination of booze, Prozac and overwhelming emotion. The next morning, I woke up in the lounge, blinked my eyes, and took in the scene. There amongst the empties was my Old Man — he'd crashed here, too. He nodded, and said: 'She's gone, mate. She's gone.'

”

I went back to work, but I was hacking around, not doing my best, not by a long shot. There's an underlying theory I have about journalism to do with the 'News Gods'. When things are going well — you're chasing an unlikely story, relying on finding someone elusive and convincing them to talk to you against all odds, and it all comes off — thank the News Gods. Because sure as hell you'll go through plenty of patches when the News Gods will abandon you — finding yourself down dead ends, not being able to get anyone to talk to you, scratching around with tip-offs that fizzle out.

As I sat at my desk in the *Herald* newsroom — the place I'd had so many lucky breaks — I knew the News Gods weren't hearing my plaintive cries. There were a couple of stories on which I made straight-out bad calls, too, where legal letters arrived in the boss's office, and lawyers were involved in a back and forth. I was not in a good space. During an interview with a senior cop, I exploded over something silly and told him to 'Get fucked!' Later, when I was political editor, I'd regularly blow up at people — but this was out of character at that time. And behaving like that towards a top policeman was incredibly bad form, obviously. If only those News Gods would shine on me.

Finally, they did, although it was in horrific circumstances, in the 'Baby Pumpkin' case. In September 2007, a guy called Nai Yin Xue strangled his wife and shoved her body into the boot of their car outside their home in Auckland. He then flew to Melbourne with their three-year-old daughter, known as Pumpkin, and abandoned her at a busy train station, leaving Australia on his own. No one knew anything until Pumpkin was found and the police pieced together what had happened. A huge international manhunt was on. Eventually, police and immigration officials figured out Xue had flown to Los Angeles.

In the middle of all this, *Herald* editor Tim Murphy strode into the newsroom and said, ‘Right, we need to get to LA.’ He looked over at me and said, ‘What are you doing, Pat?’

By the way, Tim is the only person who calls me Pat. I have no idea why. Most often I get Paddy, PG, or Patrick if people are being formal. Paddy was a family nickname from birth. For years, Patrick was the only name I used as my news byline. It was only when the programme *Paddy Gower Has Issues* came along in 2023 that I officially became ‘Paddy’ in a professional sense. But never, ever Pat. Except for Tim.

Not that I minded in this particular moment, as I was being struck by a lightning bolt from the News Gods. Next minute, photographer Greg Bowker and I were off to LA. I loved it — the hustle, the pressure, the buzz. We uncovered story after story, like talking to Xue’s martial-arts rival, and quizzing a bounty hunter about how to track people down. Xue was eventually caught and deported to New Zealand, where he was convicted of his wife’s murder in June 2009. When I look back at the work we did in LA, I see a TV reporter in the making — hatching up angles and creating highly visual, talent-driven stories.

But TV was a while off yet. I didn’t know it, but politics was to come first.

7.
INTO A SHITSTORM

I got my start in political reporting thanks to an appearance before a judge, and a conspiratorial phone call. Let's start with the judge.

In the middle of 2008, I was summoned to the High Court in Auckland. Of course, I'd been to courtrooms plenty of times by then — only that one time in the dock, back in uni days — but this was nerve-racking because the circumstances were unusual. Judges rarely gave interviews to the media. But the country's problem with methamphetamine, or P, was clogging up the High Court because there were so many cases. Judges needed help to clear the backlog, and they were getting desperate. So desperate, they needed the media.

I didn't really know why, but I got invited to the chambers of Chief High Court Judge Tony Randerson. I remember him being extremely nervous and quite highly strung about going on the record with a reporter. Early on in the interview, I paraphrased something back to him in a conversational way — I hadn't even written down a note by this stage.

He immediately reacted, throwing his hands up. 'No, no, no, no.' He was shifting in his seat and obviously thinking this was a bad idea, and was worried about being misquoted or taken out of context.

He had good reason to be nervous, because what he was doing was momentous — he was calling out politicians, encouraging them to pass a law change to help expedite the hearing of meth cases. Judges did not normally wade into Parliamentary business. The bill that would have helped was caught up in a stalemate between the government and the Opposition, and the 2008 election was fast approaching. If help didn't come soon, it was going to drag into the next year, at least.

Despite Justice Randerson's misgivings, the interview continued and the judges must have been happy because, seven weeks later, they got their wish — the bill was passed and the High Court was unclogged of P cases, which would be heard in the district courts from then on. In the weeks after it broke, the story had turned into a political to-and-fro that I'd been heavily reporting on. And someone was taking notice.

I was walking across the cart dock at the *Herald* when my mobile rang. It was *Herald* political editor Audrey Young, and she was speaking in a whispered, conspiratorial tone. I'd come to know this mode very well: when Audrey made calls about a good story, she'd lower her voice, cover her mouth as she was talking, push the phone hard against her ear, and look over her shoulder, making sure no one was listening in. She said, 'Have you ever been interested in political reporting?'

I'd been a politics student who used to read columns by John Armstrong, so of course there must have been a trace of interest there. But the truth was I'd never thought about covering politics as a journalist, and in my time as a shit-kicking crime reporter I'd come to think journos from the 'gallery' were a bit pompous.

Audrey pressed on: 'There might be a temporary job coming up in the Press Gallery covering the election.' The Press Gallery was a special club of journalists who worked in Parliament. Membership needed to be approved by the Speaker of the House, and it came with privileges like a Parliamentary swipe card; the main news organisations had offices within the precinct itself. All the journalists were boxed in together, working alongside each other within the most hyper-competitive journalistic habitat in the country. I certainly liked the idea of the hyper-competitive part. Audrey pushed on with her hushed sales pitch: 'I've been watching your stories and I think you'd be good.' She was particularly impressed with the yarn on the judges.

The reason she was being conspiratorial was that the bosses had offered her another couple of reporters as options for this role, but not me, and she wanted to sound me out. I thought, *You know what? I need a change, so why not?* Audrey concocted a jiggery-pokery plan where I'd put my hand up for this job that I wasn't meant to know was going — without mentioning I'd spoken to her, of course. It was my first political backroom deal. And it worked.

Soon afterwards, aged 31, I was standing on the steps of Parliament in a suit and shiny shoes as a proud member of the *New Zealand Herald* Press Gallery team, temporarily at least.

Little did I know at the time, I wouldn't be leaving this

building for ten years. That day, I was full of hope and excitement, looking forward to holding the powerful to account and questioning those who ran the country. But there would be times to come when I would instead be questioning myself, broken and wondering if I could carry on, asking why the hell I'd ever set foot in the place.

”

That was all ahead of me. I was escorted to my little desk in our little office, surrounded by the detritus of government announcements and scandals of days gone by, manila folders stuffed with old press releases, towers of old Budget documents, and the obligatory 'who's who of Parliament' poster on the walls. And there were John Armstrong and Audrey Young, two of the most brilliant political journalists ever. John was an oracle, a political genius who understood power, and could detect the smallest shift in which party or which figure had control. To me, he was like the Yoda of political journalism.

There was another aspect to John that made him heroic in my eyes. By the time I arrived in Wellington in 2008, he was well and truly in the grip of severe Parkinson's disease. It was physically debilitating and he found it hard to get around. I was sitting next to him one day at a press conference when he had some kind of seizure. I ran back to the office to get his pills, so full of fear for him.

Plenty of other people would have given up the job, but against the odds John fought and fought, his formidable brain desperately trying to outlast his failing body. He died in 2022, aged 68, a true GOAT of journalism (Greatest of All Time). It was one of the biggest honours of my career to work alongside him.

”

As a gallery newbie, I counted myself damn lucky to have John and Audrey as mentors. But there was no time for sentiment or pep talks — I'd walked straight into a shitstorm. But it was the best kind of shitstorm, a political shitstorm that Audrey herself had whipped up.

Audrey had broken an almighty yarn about donations to New Zealand First. Have you ever seen photos or footage of Winston Peters holding up a big 'NO' sign at a press conference, one of the most iconic images of New Zealand politics? He had that sign made in response to Audrey's story over a certain donation. Other journalists were on the case now, too, and a full-on war was raging between Peters and the media — not the first, not the last — and I was ordered to charge straight into the firing line. Audrey had ideas for me to chase up, millions of angles and tips to follow. On day one, I was dispatched along the underground travelator that runs from the Beehive to Bowen House on Lambton Quay, and off to a meeting in downtown Wellington with Sir Bob Jones about another donation.

Another time, Peters cornered me in an airport and asked 'Who's your snout?' (meaning who's my source) after I broke a yarn about New Zealand First. It was all on, and I thought, *Shit, this is awesome!* The adrenaline, the rush — it was unreal.

I'd always viewed the gallery like a special club, but it wasn't until I got to Wellington that I really appreciated what that meant. There was always a feeling of journalistic gravitas about it, a mystique. Many of the big household names of New Zealand journalism had trod its corridors — Bill Ralston, Richard Long, Linda Clark, Mark Sainsbury, Jane Young, Richard Harman, Barry Soper, John Campbell. Each year, there was a photo taken — like a school photo — and hung on the wall, so you could see almost everyone who'd worked there. It was like a rogues' gallery, and the fashion choices on show made it bloody funny.

When I started, Guyon Espiner and Duncan Garner were the political editors for TVNZ and *3News*, respectively, and to me they seemed almost unreal characters. Yet on the first night, we went for a drink and there they were sitting with us having a beer. The bar, by the way, was inside the Beehive — everyone called it 3.2 because it was the second door on the third floor. I couldn't believe it — you didn't even need to leave the place to get a drink. I remember thinking, *How good!*

Parliament was like a village, hermetically sealed from the rest of the world. Everything you needed was there. Once you got to work, the only time you left was to follow politicians, and then you'd often be travelling together with them in a van or an air-force plane.

Everything and everyone was interconnected. The government, the Opposition, the smaller parties, all these officials and the Press Gallery — scheming and plotting like characters in a tactical board game. Now I was in it, too, and I was one of the little players, watching on as one of the big players, Audrey, was taking on a giant, Peters, who was Minister of Foreign Affairs and in government with Helen Clark. I was all in.

In the early days, it was the straight competition, the

adrenaline, the action that attracted me to the job. For me it wasn't *I'm watching politics in action.* It was *This is fun, this is aggressive, this is a test.* You needed to outwit the politicians, and outwit the other journalists to beat them to the yarn.

Dealing with Peters from the get-go made that tricky. We'd quickly moved into covering the election campaign, and Audrey had me following Peters around. There was weird story after weird story. For instance, in a TV interview he flatly denied ever using a helicopter to campaign, but I had a picture and some video of him with helicopters from the 1999 and 2005 campaigns. He responded by saying he'd used helicopters for travel, not campaigning. Classic Peters.

Things were unravelling for him at that time, with John Key saying he wouldn't work with New Zealand First if National won. On election night 2008 I was in Tauranga, where Peters lost to future National leader Simon Bridges. And with New Zealand First not getting across the 5 per cent threshold, Peters was out of Parliament — not for the first time, and not the last.

Our media contingent waited for him to arrive at his party headquarters, but he stayed for only a couple of minutes, ignored the cameras, danced with one of his supporters, and then headed upstairs to a non-smoking room. He let only one journalist in for an interview — someone from a small community radio station, just to rark everyone else up. I was outside in the hallway; all I got to see was the door open slightly as the smell of cigarette smoke wafted out.

John Key was to blame for me staying on as a political reporter, because when he won the 2008 election it triggered staff movements that got me a permanent job in the gallery. After a change of government, there is always a whopping tidal flow in Wellington, a great migration of people — into the Beehive, out of the Beehive, into Parliament, out of Parliament, into the Press Gallery, out of the Press Gallery. One of my colleagues, Paula Oliver, was headhunted to work for Key, so a full-time vacancy opened up in the *Herald* office. There wasn't really a discussion about it or an interview; at the end of work one day after I'd filed a story, Audrey said, 'Good news — you've got the job.' I was locked in.

There were so many stories to chase, with new Cabinet ministers asserting their authority, shaking up departments that had operated for nine years under a Labour government, and Key inheriting some thorny problems that had been around for a while. One of those was Afghanistan.

Clark had committed New Zealand soldiers to Afghanistan back at the time of the US-led invasion in 2001, initially sending in the SAS. They had since been withdrawn and New Zealand's contribution was a Provincial Reconstruction Team based in the central province of Bamiyan. Key was coming under pressure from the US to send the SAS back.

As part of the campaign to ramp up support for its plan for a surge in Afghanistan, the US State Department arranged for journalists from around the world to go to the warzone and be briefed. Via the US Embassy in Wellington, I was given the opportunity to go to NATO headquarters in Brussels, then into Afghanistan.

Beforehand, I was scared shitless — I'd never been to a warzone. A mate who was in the SAS and had fought in Afghanistan met me for a beer at the Backbencher pub and I was hoping he'd reassure me. 'If things get heavy, and there're shots being fired, just get low, Paddy, get as low as you can,' he told me. I wasn't reassured.

When I landed in Singapore in transit on the way there, I'd worked myself into such a state I rang the embassy worker who'd arranged the trip. I wasn't crying, exactly, but I was upset. 'I want to come back.' There was no coming back, and, of course, in the end I was perfectly safe — there was no way the US was going to let a bunch of journalists who were in Afghanistan at their invitation get blown up. But I was so naive and inexperienced.

I was taken to a training ground for Afghan police, just ordinary guys going out into the Taliban's firing line. They were being trained by American cops, not soldiers, and, even worse, they were training with imitation guns, not real ones. It was horrifying and I was scared for them.

The biggest story from the trip came when we had a short interview with the US Ambassador to NATO, who was quite a big deal in the scheme of things. I asked him why New Zealand should give more, and he said New Zealand should front up because there could come a time when it needed its allies to stand by its side. I remember thinking, *Shit mate, interesting call. That won't go down that well back home.* The front-page headline read: 'US: Fight for us, you may need us.' It looked like the Yanks were pressuring us, which they no doubt were, but of course both Washington and Wellington were pretending they weren't. The American plan to get me to write positive stuff about the war had kind of backfired, but hey, the ambassador said it.

A story that did not make the paper was a party put on by some American diplomats in Kabul. Earlier in the day, I'd met up with a couple of Kiwis who were serving there, and I'd said, 'Oh, hey, there's a party tonight, why don't you guys come? We could have a beer together.' They looked at each other sideways — I didn't realise that their tour of duty was a dry trip. No alcohol. I sure as hell wasn't going to tell anyone. So along they came.

I hadn't drunk much during the trip either, and Kabul is at 1800 metres altitude (Wellington is at 10 metres), which does strange things to your metabolism. I was feeling pretty blazed after a couple of beers. I looked around and — uh, oh. One of the Kiwi guys was absolutely hammered. We quietly ushered him out of there before there were any dramas.

”

After the initial thrill of just bashing out yarns in the gallery, I became more interested in the politics itself. As the Parliamentary term ticked by, parties were already preparing for the next time around at the ballot box. And in Auckland Central there was a showdown looming. It became known as the 'Battle of the Babes', a title I've been blamed for, but for which I say the provenance is disputed.

Auckland Central's incumbent MP was its rising star National's Nikki Kaye, and she was about to be challenged by a Labour MP who had entered Parliament in 2008 by the name of Jacinda Ardern. It was a good story and I was on it.

The following remains a hotly disputed series of events, but when it came time to write the story there was a lot of back and forth in the office, and then a decision was made with Audrey to call it the 'Battle of the Babes'. It was immediately problematic — so much so that the headline was changed online within hours after an outcry. To be clear, I agree it was a deeply sexist headline, of course. If there was any point in mitigation to be made, the original intent was that it was a reference to *Babes in the Wood*, an expression derived from a traditional children's tale from Ye Olde England referencing innocents wandering into a dangerous situation — rather than 'babes' as in attractive women.

But anyway, it went through in print, in black and white, under my byline — by Patrick Gower.

Years later, it was still problematic — particularly when it was brought up as if I'd done it as *Newshub* political editor, rather than as a junior political reporter at the *Herald*.

My memory was that it was a joint decision and Audrey approved it — at the time all my stories were still signed off by Audrey. Nothing went out of that office without her say-so. She disputed this and even threw me under the bus in a column years later, distancing herself from it. I still say she was involved; in fact, to this day I reckon she initially came up with it. We've had a lot of banter about it over the years, and no doubt will for years to come.

Ardern most certainly did not engage in banter over it — far from it. In a *Spinoff* interview with Toby Manhire years later, after she became prime minister, the subject came up, and Manhire reported her response like this: '"That was Patrick Gower in the *Herald*," she says, with a death stare.'

”

Every now and then the News Gods shone on me and I could break a decent yarn doing bugger-all work. One day I was in the office and there was a sliding-door moment when my colleague Claire Trevett handed me a cracking story that changed the trajectory of my career — and my life. She'd discovered that ACT leader Rodney Hide — who'd made a name for himself as a perkbuster, exposing MPs and officials for wasteful spending — had used $25,000 of taxpayer money taking his girlfriend on an overseas tour. Basically, the perkbuster had been busted for perks.

Claire had uncovered this in some public documents, but there was an important announcement at the Treasury at the same time and just the two of us working. Knowing that I probably didn't even know where the Treasury was, let alone how to report on it, Claire threw herself on the grenade. It meant she didn't have time to finish the Hide story — she was worried another journo would get the yarn — so it was handed to me to finish off. I got a response from Hide, and the story went straight to the front page of the *Herald* the next day, where I referred to him as a 'former perkbuster'. It had one of the key ingredients for a hot political yarn — hypocrisy. It blew up into a decent political shitstorm, and I've always felt stink for Claire, as I should have put her byline on it with mine. At that time, good stories in the morning papers set the news agenda for the whole day. And this was a hell of a yarn — both the TVNZ and *3News* political editors assigned one of their reporters to follow it up.

One of those political editors was Duncan Garner, from *3News*. I bumped into him in the corridor that morning, and he said to me: 'Great story — come and work for me.' He had a vacancy, and he wanted me to take the spot. Everything changed, almost in an instant. Television — which I'd never, ever thought was an option for me — beckoned.

8.
ATTACK DOG

I was offered the usual employment contract to join *3News*, but there was also a separate contract, an altogether off-the-books one. After Duncan hit me up about a job, things got rolling quickly, as was his way. But I was anxious — frankly, I'd seen other print reporters come across to TV and they'd looked like crap.

But Duncan's approach got me thinking about the future of the media industry — I thought things didn't look good for the *Herald*, whereas TV networks would be fine, surely. (History would prove me quite wrong on this.)

Duncan was persistent; once he got something in his head, he could be incredibly persuasive. I took a full-on hammering from him; he turned into some kind of cult leader trying to persuade me to join his sect, not letting any other thoughts enter my mind, surrounding me with how good it would be, promising that nothing could go wrong.

One hot summer's day near the end of 2009, we traipsed around to the back of Parliament, to a semi-secret spot called the

Speaker's Lawn. It was somewhere not many people could see you. Duncan was pressing me. 'What are you worried about, PG? What do you need, PG?' So I told him: 'Look, DG, I'm worried I'll fail.' He stared at me silently for a while, which was highly unusual for him. Then he said: 'I won't let you fail. I'll have your back. I promise you, I'll have your back.' He grabbed a piece of paper and we wrote it down — he put on paper this side-contract saying how he'd never let me fail, how he'd teach me everything he knew. Things to reassure me. The Garner Contract.

Duncan was like a hurricane at that time, the dominant political journalist. He had a swag of big stories to his name, and a collection of scalps — holding to account ministers and officials who had messed up. In that regard, he was far and away the best. His type of television journalism was changing the game — he'd created a high-octane, in-your-face style backed by strong opinion and analysis. I looked at him in awe and thought I'd never be able to emulate him. But here was a chance to be his understudy. So we shook hands and the deal was done.

”

Despite the deal, despite the contract and the promises — which Duncan lived up to — I cannot put into words how hard it was to change from print journo to TV journo. There were a whole bunch of logistical and technical things I had to get to grips with. In print, you rang people up, got a comment, then wrote a story. In TV, you had to convince them to go on camera, interview them, get shots to go with it, record your piece to camera, go back to the office and sit with the editor and put it all together —

there was just so much faffing about compared to print. Working in print was like using a scalpel, whereas in TV it was like being handed an axe — it was blunt but very powerful.

Also, I'd never done anything performance-related before. I'd never been in school plays or done anything where my voice had been recorded. I hadn't studied television. I'd never worn make-up, and now I was having to put on my own make-up. And as soon as I got near the camera, it was like I was allergic to it. It was a hundred times harder than I thought it was going to be. Really basic things were hard to start with: like at the end of a story when I signed off, I was supposed to say, 'Patrick Gower, *3News.*' Every reporter signed off with their name. But I couldn't even say that properly. I mumbled it. I remember newsreader Carolyn Robinson trying to help me: 'Oh, you're supposed to do it like this.' And I'd repeat it, thinking I'd nailed it. Blank stare. 'Try again.'

However, *3News* being *3News*, I was live on air in my first week. It was a lean, mean organisation so people were thrown in the deep end, and let me tell you it did not get much deeper than going live on the six o'clock news. And I stood out — as the Kiwi proverbial saying goes — like dog's balls. Whereas other reporters had come through the ranks, working on morning shows and late-night shows, slowly learning the performance aspect and having voice training — I'd done none of that. I was straight on the main bulletin.

Then of course there were my looks. I did not look like a classic TV reporter — a clean-cut, handsome young man. I was an unusual-looking dude. I was lucky social media hadn't really kicked off. But it didn't take long for me to see and hear negative comments. 'What's he doing on TV?' 'He's so useless.' 'How can TV3 let this guy on air?' There was a website called Throng (it's long gone now) that reviewed TV, including the first break of both main bulletins every night — and I took an absolute hammering. I found it humiliating because I knew it was well followed in the industry and every TV reporter was reading it.

What I didn't know at the time was that Duncan and my other bosses, Wellington bureau chief Gordon McBride and head of news Mark Jennings, were shielding me from a lot. There were complaints coming into the switchboard, and there were even people within *3News* wondering why I was there.

While I was being protected from much of it, I only needed to see one comment to make me doubt myself and shake my resolve to do the job. It started to have a profound effect, particularly one comment that kept coming up: 'He's so ugly.' It had been a while since I had been confronted by this stuff. At school, of course, I'd been extremely self-conscious about my looks, and had gone through teasing and bullying. But as I'd grown older, gone to university and become a print reporter, that stuff just tapered off. My looks were irrelevant. All of a sudden, all those feelings, all that hurt, all those taunts, were back because I was on TV. And it was more brutal than at school because it was coming from the general public. I was an adult and it was my job.

The comments about my performance, that I was useless — I accepted those. But the ones about how I looked? They really got inside my head. Because, in all my calculations about coming to TV, I just hadn't contemplated this would happen. How naive. Because people made comments about TV presenters' and reporters' looks all the time. Growing up, I'd heard family members talk about people on TV. 'I can't stand her voice' or 'he's weird-looking'. All of a sudden, I was thinking, *Shit, that's me. I'm the guy whose looks everyone is talking about?* On Christmas Day, coming up to a year on the telly, one of my cousins turned to me after a few beers and said, 'I can't watch you on TV — it's too embarrassing.' He wasn't trying to be mean, and the beers had loosened his tongue, but it was shattering. *Oh my God — even my own family think this?* I felt like I did at school when the older kids would say something — the colour just faded out of everything.

TV is a confidence game, so it became a vicious circle. Because I was self-conscious, because I was looking in the mirror and worrying about what people thought about my looks, my performance got worse and worse. Duncan could see what was going on, and he was doing his best, and so, too, was our Wellington boss Gordon 'Flash' McBride, a grizzly teddy bear of a man and a TV3 legend. He was an old-school newsman from central casting, a journo to his bones, who came from print to TV back in the day, too. From day one, Gordon looked after me, and became like my work dad, someone I went to for advice. He became incredibly important to my career.

Gordon was a real hard-arse, and Duncan was, too, so it wasn't like we sat around having millennial-style chats about how I was feeling. But Gordon had this big office with a couch in it and he'd be in there with his feet up on the desk and if you walked in with questions or not feeling right, he'd spring up. He'd open a bottle of red wine like clockwork at four o'clock on a Friday and you'd chew the fat and feel reassured.

But it was most certainly not a kumbaya-style workplace. Gordon and Duncan fought about stories all the time, which made me feel awkward, like Mum and Dad were arguing. Those were the days when journos told each other to 'get fucked' or 'fuck off' and slammed the phone down, stuff you'd never get away with today. One time, Duncan and I were having a disagreement about how we should do something and he said, 'Okay, there's only one way to settle this.' I thought he was going to say 'coin toss', but he said 'scrum'.

We were in the *3News* gallery office in our suits and next thing we were packing down like a couple of rugby forwards. I was lanky, like a lock, drawing on my Fourth XV experience. Duncan told everyone he was a halfback at Westlake Boys High School — and he definitely had the mouth of a halfback. But he'd taken on the body shape of a front-rower and had the low centre of gravity to do the job. We were straight into it, he put on a huge push, I was trying to get low to recover lost ground, but he propelled me backwards. We were barrelling straight towards a big, old fax machine against the wall — an unstoppable force with a combined weight of probably 180 kilograms. Next thing, we smashed the fax into smithereens and I was sitting on top of a pile of broken plastic with Duncan on top of me. 'Oh, well,' he said, 'looks like we're doing it my way, PG.'

Through the rough and tumble of the office, the rough and tumble of the criticism, Duncan and Gordon never, ever let me think there was anything wrong. They just formed a security blanket around me, with positive reinforcement, and motivated me to get out there and crack on.

As part of my schooling in TV political reporting, they sent me on a trip around the Pacific — Foreign Minister Murray McCully and a few MPs, including Shane Jones, were visiting

ABOVE Bursting in to break some news. I clearly liked playing the crowd from an early age.

LEFT I was a backyard dreamer, playing all sorts of make-believe. Here I am in one of my favourite roles: a commando outwitting an imaginary invading force.

RIGHT I got big buck teeth early on, and with them came the nickname 'Paddy Carrots'.

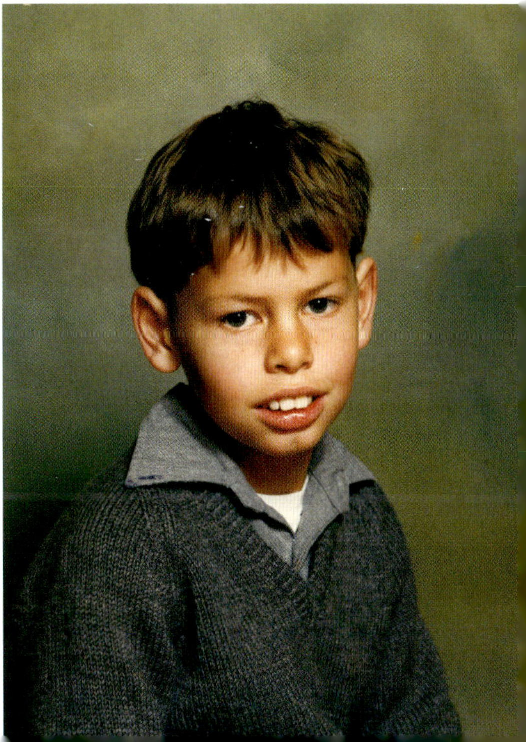

ABOVE The photo of me and New Plymouth mayor David Lean that appeared on the front page of the *Taranaki Herald* in March 1989, with the headline 'Who's the boss?' The story describes me turning a school visit into a coup against the mayor, donning his mayoral cloak and chain and climbing atop a bench to make an announcement. Talk about a sign of things to come. *Stuff Limited / Susan Welch / Puke Ariki*

RIGHT Me and the Old Man, 1991 (I'm fourteen). With braces, acne and changing facial features, I had a lot going on in my teenage years.

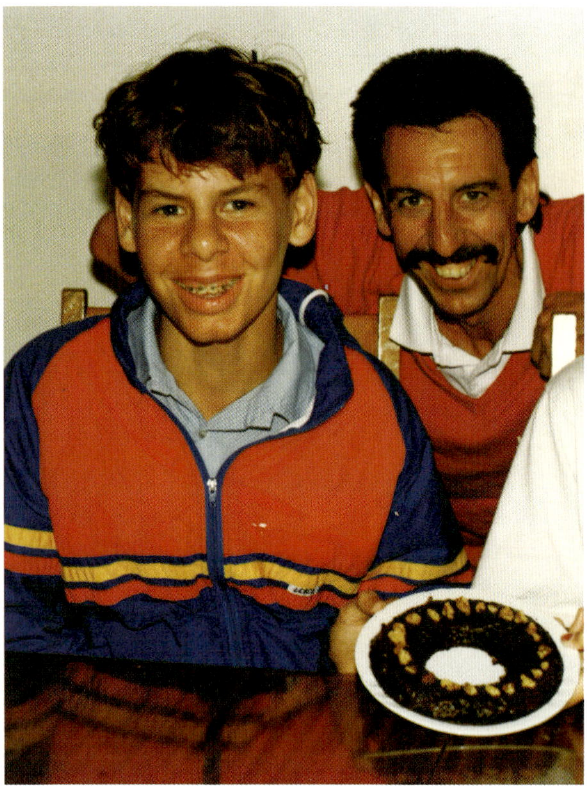

LEFT Binge drinking was part of my weekly routine as a teenager. My mate Dion and I are around sixteen years old in this shot. Dion is the guy I would famously sidestep on the way to a momentous try in a school rugby match, so cheers to that!

BELOW A very special photo with my mum, about a year before she died. This was taken in the very early days of her cancer. I don't like to look at photos of her after this time; it was all downhill. This is the way I like to remember her.

ABOVE In Afghanistan on assignment in 2009. The war was heating up and so was I. I'm pretty fresh here, quite naive and absolutely shitting myself.

OPPOSITE TOP With Prime Minister John Key moments after the infamous 'Washington Choke', 2014 (see page 121). *New Zealand Government*

RIGHT Stretched out with my boom mike, in prime position to capture the convo between Prime Minister John Key and US President Barack Obama in the White House, 2014. *New Zealand Government*

ABOVE With Barry Soper on the beach in Dubai before going into Iraq in 2015 — these were the happy hours before my passport debacle unfolded (see page 129).

LEFT A shot taken from inside the Chinook helicopter that was carrying us across Iraq in a sandstorm; it shows a US Air Force Apache attack helicopter flying alongside us. Camera operator Cam Williams broke the rules to take this photo after an SAS soldier got sick of hearing us argue over whether to do it or not! *Cam Williams*

RIGHT With Gordon McBride, my 'Work Dad', a great mentor and friend. He paid me the great honour of requesting me as a pallbearer at his funeral. It took a few years but I found a way to pay him back.

OPPOSITE Getting pumped up for my live cross into the 6 p.m. news, 2015. It was always a big way to end a big day reporting on Parliament. *North & South / Nicola Edmonds*

TOP Face to face with Donald Trump as he takes my question during a press conference at his Mar-a-Lago estate on Super Tuesday, 2016. Trump was on his way to becoming US President, while I wasn't even meant to be in the room! *Newshub*

ABOVE All smiles with Winston Peters after the 2017 election, when he was holding the balance of power. I can virtually guarantee that Peters would have been ripping into me in some way, and of course dodging my question.

leaders around the islands. It was a chance to learn how to cover stories overseas and also get to know some of the politicians better. On the trip, there was free alcohol on board the air-force flights and, being a boozer from way back, I was in my element. Except it took a toll. One day I was so rancidly hungover I struggled to work, even though we were in Kiribati, a country hardly anybody gets to go to. We filmed a kid struggling to find clean drinking water, the first time I'd seen such abject poverty. But as soon as we were back on the plane, I hooked straight back into the Central Otago pinot noir. I drank so much one day I stumbled coming down the stairs off the plane and nearly fell. Even years later, air-force staff reminded me about that. It was humiliating, but it didn't stop me. There was frequent big drinking back in Wellington, too. After a tough day — drink. After a big day — drink. After a big story — drink.

One of those big stories, which stirred a heap of controversy, began with the Labour MP Chris Carter, who had racked up a whole lot of stuff on his taxpayer-funded credit card when he was a minister. Labour was now in Opposition and it was a brewing shitstorm. The Press Gallery descended. We were all waiting outside the Labour caucus room to ask questions and he wouldn't front. Usually these things were settled by the person under scrutiny stepping out and answering a couple of questions, then away they'd go.

Not Carter. Suddenly he dashed out of the room and didn't stop. He pushed past the pack, then nipped down the stairwell. It was a clever move. Everyone was startled. I was with Cam Williams, a *3News* camera operator. We didn't say anything to each other but we just decided we were going after Carter.

We tore down the stairs after him, down two flights, Carter looking over his shoulder at us. Cam was filming the whole time, despite how dangerous it is running down stairs with your eye pressed to a camera. Carter bolted into a colleague's office, so we thought we were back to standing around waiting for him. But it turned out the MP he'd sought refuge from didn't like him and told him to get out, because next thing Carter was through the door and we were right on his tail again. He got to the famous black and white tiles in the Parliamentary foyer and swept around in a circle, looking over his shoulder at us tucked in behind him, filming, asking questions. I was wondering where he was going to go or if we'd be stuck in this three-person whirlpool in the foyer of Parliament forever. He eventually figured out a path to safety — boom, he shot into the debating chamber where all the MPs sat, one place we knew was an absolute no-go for us. The chase was over.

It was TV gold, but we'd broken a bunch of rules. There were certain places you were allowed to film MPs, and places you weren't — the stairways being one of them, especially when you were chasing MPs. Duncan and Gordon watched the footage. Duncan loved it because he was in a pitched battle with Carter at the time — he wanted a scalp. And Gordon had a bit of a reckless streak, so he was keen, too, and said: 'Fuck it, let's run it.'

When it played on the news, politicians went apoplectic — there were complaints and demands for me to be stripped of my Press Gallery membership, or at least be suspended. Duncan and Gordon were called before the Speaker, Lockwood Smith, and got a bollocking, but they managed to make a plea bargain on my behalf and I was allowed to stay. The deal was that *3News* lost its car-parking privileges for a month instead. I was off the hook and back in the game, where I was starting to build a reputation as a maverick, of going right up to the line for a story — and sometimes over it.

There was another infamous moment, involving Don Brash, who was leader of the ACT Party in the lead-up to the 2011 election. I'd chased after him, camera rolling, through a hotel lobby, and out to the foyer where he went to get into a taxi, then said to me, in the politest way: 'Patrick, you're a deceitful bastard, quite frankly, and I don't want to talk to you anymore.'

The incident, and others, provoked a column from former newspaper editor Karl du Fresne, who wrote: 'Gower has obviously been designated TV3's resident attack dog, with a brief to get in politicians' faces . . . To goad the almost painfully polite Brash into responding so vehemently must have taken some doing, but I bet Gower went home that night feeling pleased with his day's work.' Du Fresne was right — I did go home happy that night. I'd made a moment of television, I'd rattled a senior politician. Although, despite what du Fresne believed, Brash may have been a polite man but he did snap easily that day. It didn't take a lot for him to call me a deceitful bastard.

The incident fed into this narrative that Duncan and I were practitioners of a type of political journalism that was aggressive, confrontational and take-no-prisoners. Which is exactly what we were.

In the heat of the 2011 campaign, a story broke that came to be known as the 'Teapot Tapes'. ACT needed to win a seat to stay in Parliament and had come to an agreement with National in the Epsom electorate, where National would deliberately let them through, in what I'd call a 'dirty deal'. Two weeks before polling day, ACT candidate John Banks and National leader John Key met in a cafe — a staged moment in front of the cameras, a way of Key tacitly endorsing Banks and giving National voters in Epsom the nod and wink that they should vote for Banks as their electorate MP. During the meeting, a freelance camera operator left his recording device on the table and the conversation was captured on tape. Both Key and Banks claimed the conversation was private and shouldn't be made public.

Duncan set about desperately trying to find out what was on the tape. Like I said, when Duncan put his mind to stuff, it usually happened. And it wasn't long before he rang me: 'Well, PG, I've got the tape.' I went and saw him and he was holding a piece of paper with five or six lines, bullet points of the tape's contents that he'd typed out. It was probably the most important piece of paper in the country at that moment, so precious it seemed to be glowing. I read a line from Key saying Winston Peters and New Zealand First, who were voted out in 2008, were not going to get back in because his supporters were 'dying out'. It was explosive. Duncan went into his serious mode, which was always kind of scary as he looked a little psycho. He said: 'Tomorrow is going to be the biggest day of your career. I'm going to go and get Key and you are going to get Banks. Our job is to tip this campaign upside down.' They were his orders.

The next day, I was on the hunt, trying to find Banks. I couldn't find him. Meanwhile, Duncan ambushed Key with a two-camera operation. I still had nothing. Where was Banks? I later found out that Wayne Eagleson, Key's chief of staff and right-hand-man, had told Banks to go to ground and that whatever he did, he shouldn't go near a TV camera.

But Banks loved the camera and he couldn't help himself. Eventually, I got a phone call from Banks. 'Meet me in the Auckland Domain.' The stage was set for a bizarre, enthralling exchange. He didn't know that I knew what was on the tape. We started filming, and I told him I knew and held up a piece of paper with the bullet points. Banks came back with some theatrical answers and did an almost comical interview in which he started talking in the third person. 'John Banks has never been a loser, John Banks doesn't like losing', and so on. It was incredibly poor politics but made incredibly good television.

Duncan and I had done our jobs — tipping the campaign upside down. Duncan had a couple of sayings he really liked. He'd call a yarn that wasn't so great a 'shitbox yarn' (invariably one by our competitors). For a good yarn, usually his, he'd just say 'bang', or 'baaaaang'. Duncan rang me, and his first words were 'boomy baaaang'. I remember the adrenaline surging through my system that night — I couldn't sleep. It was electrifying. The next day I was in Tauranga interviewing Peters — with all the controversy, his campaign had been revived — and I did a piece to camera saying this could bring him back into Parliament. It proved to be on the money: Peters re-emerged victorious on election night.

I also scored a victory of my own on election night. I was assigned to cover the National Party campaign at SkyCity. As was tradition, TVNZ and *3News* tossed a coin to decide who was going to get the first live TV interview with Key after he'd spoken to the crowd from the stage. My producer Sarah Hall, who had done a few election nights and was old-school TV3, absolutely hated losing to TVNZ and was desperate to win the toss, banging on about how she'd never lost the toss in previous elections. Then she lost the toss.

So we hatched another plan. While everyone was waiting upstairs for Key, we snuck downstairs with a camera and looked out for his car. The studio crossed to us when we saw him pull up, he hopped out of the car, and before anyone knew it, I was interviewing Key live on air as he walked into the venue, which was a good 500 metres away and enough time for a decent live interview. I couldn't believe it — it was a massive scoop. It was a classic *3News* underdog, pulling-victory-from-the-jaws-of-defeat moment. Back at the newsroom, all the *3News* originals — the guys who thrived on the rivalry with TVNZ — were pumped. I remember them cheering when I arrived, and coming up and congratulating me. I really was one of the crew now. I didn't know it at the time, but they were watching closely over at TVNZ, too, and I was about to get an intriguing phone call from one of their top dogs.

9.
BECOMING 'POL ED'

There was no time for a cup of tea after the 2011 campaign, as things were changing in the gallery. Guyon Espiner was leaving as TVNZ political editor, jumping ship to TV3 to work in current affairs. I got a call from a TVNZ boss 'strongly encouraging' me to apply for the job. I initially thought it was a prank call as I wasn't thinking about becoming a 'Pol Ed', the gallery's nickname for those who ascended to political editors. But TVNZ was serious, and I was tossing up what to do when another opportunity suddenly arose. Duncan Garner wanted out of the gallery, too.

He was keen to move into radio and television-presenting in Auckland and was negotiating hard with Mark Jennings, who was trying to get Duncan to hold off. In the middle of all this, I was called to lunch at Logan Brown in Wellington with Duncan, Jennings and the chief executive at the time, Sussan Turner. This was a new world to me; I'd never been to lunch with the bosses like this, I'd never had to do any corporate schmoozing. So I was sitting there, too nervous to speak much, just nodding and smiling as it all unfolded, and trying not to spill anything on the crisp, white linen tablecloths.

What was being concocted was a succession plan because, although Jennings was keen for me to take over, there was no way I was ready and he wanted Duncan to stay until I was. I was presented with a contract, whereby Duncan stayed for a year, and I'd take over from him as political editor after that. Just like that, out of nowhere. It was basically: 'Here's a promotion, here's a pay rise — congratulations.' It was surreal. I was like, 'Oh, yep. Okay. Thanks.' It was momentous. I made an excuse to go to the bathroom, and took it all in. *What. The. Fuck?*

It was also the beginning of an extremely stressful twelve months of mounting tension between Duncan and me. It felt to me that he was bitter about having to stay and he sometimes reminded me he was only there because of me. At the same time, I was keen to get on with the job and assert myself, while he wanted to make as big a splash as he could before heading out the door. I had to follow his orders and I didn't always want to. It got incredibly tetchy.

It was so difficult to be working that way — he was a friend and mentor — but we were two massive egos in a tiny office. Mentally, I found it tough. I'd been off Prozac for a few years, and things had been good. Or so I thought. But I'd gone through huge changes in a short space of time, from a temporary assignment in the Press Gallery for the *Herald* to the political editor-in-waiting for *3News*. Rising responsibility, rising profile, rising pressure. There was also stuff with Mum I hadn't dealt with, and all the stuff about my looks. I was swept up in a wave of working and drinking, working and drinking, non-stop. I was just obsessed with chasing yarns, and I don't ever remember turning down going for a drink. Now there was pressure on me to be political editor, and I wanted it, but I wasn't ready. Duncan and I were clashing and there were mind games going on.

My brain started feeling like it was being wrung out. Squeeze, squeeze, squeeze. So I decided to see a psychologist, secretly. She had a place near Parliament and I would sneak in there, not wanting to be clocked in the waiting room. Working with her was really helpful and gave me some relief. But I didn't stick around for long; after a few sessions I felt better and stopped going. I wasn't keen to look under the PG bonnet. Besides, I had stuff to do, Duncan (temporarily) to comply with, and yarns of my own to break.

"

My time in Parliament had coincided with Helen Clark getting voted out in 2008 and the Labour Party descending into what could only be described as an epic meltdown. Year four of the meltdown was in 2012. I loved covering Labour, drawing on a rich vein of sources right throughout the party, from MPs to the unions to apparatchiks. And I knew the constitution inside out, which came in handy leading up to the 2012 annual conference.

David Shearer had not been leader for long but there were already major ructions. Another David — Cunliffe — was manoeuvring in the background, and there was a move underway within the party to change the way the leader was elected, giving a bigger voice to the wider membership, where Cunliffe was more popular than Shearer.

At party conferences, the Saturday was usually a bit of drudgery for the media, but at this conference, it was all on. There was an uprising from the party faithful against the caucus, many of whom had formed an ABC camp — Anyone But Cunliffe. I was watching what was going on and it was electrifying — raw politics right in front of me. Some senior members and Shearer loyalists were trying to dissuade people from change, but more and more speeches were supporting this rearguard action from the membership and there was a boil-over coming. I was glued to everything, watching Cunliffe like a hawk because if the vote went through, he was in the box seat to challenge for the leadership within months.

The second the remit passed, I was in his face. Cunliffe wasn't even out of his seat and I was there with my camera and microphone, getting to him before he'd processed what had gone on. Cunliffe tried to dance around my questions, so I went straight at him. 'I couldn't be clearer — I'm asking you to rule out having a go at the leadership.' Cunliffe: 'This is a constitutional conference, not a leadership conference.' We went on, thump, thwack, boom . . . it was blow after blow as we slugged it out. Enthralling political theatre and great TV. I felt like I was busting through, developing my own style, operating in what I would come to call 'the ninety-ninth percentile' — my top level. It was a place I aimed to be in whenever it really mattered. Really getting into the zone, focusing on the story and what was going to make it compelling. I was showing I was ready to be Pol Ed.

But I still had Duncan to contend with. He was desperate to

get a hit before he left the gallery. He latched onto a story that Labour had put him onto, alleging there was a recording of John Key speaking about his nemesis at the time, Kim Dotcom, during a visit to the spy agency, the Government Communications Security Bureau. It was complex and flimsy. But Duncan sensed it was going to be his last big scoop. I got sent off to do the dirty work, which was to confront Key about it. I was none too happy because my days of doing Duncan's dirty work were about a month from being over, and here I was doing one of the dirtiest jobs of all — door-stepping Key and trying to catch him out over some tenuous allegations. It only made Key grumpy, snippy and suspicious with me, right before I was due to take over as political editor.

It made me think of Duncan's phrase for an average yarn, a 'shitbox yarn'. Well, this was a shitbox yarn if ever there was one, and I was stuck in the middle of it, having this awkward interview with the Prime Minister. I wanted Duncan to go out on a big yarn, but this wasn't it. But Duncan being Duncan, he managed to spin the shitbox yarn around and put pressure back on Shearer's leadership because the evidence was so flimsy. Duncan turned his failed hit-job on Key into a hit-job on Shearer, and it was an alright yarn after all. He really was a master; I couldn't help but admire him as he went out the door with his little grin on his face.

”

Finally, I was running the show. I started with a purge to cleanse Duncan from the office. I emptied out his desk. There was a curtain next to where he sat, and behind it on the windowsill was a stack of dinner plates, each with a fork and a bit of tomato sauce — a pile he'd been building there for God knows how long. There was a red high-heel shoe under the desk, among all sorts of shit. I wanted it all gone.

On my first day at the wheel, I called a team meeting at the Ministry of Food Cafe near Parliament. We were a relatively inexperienced team: Brook Sabin, who was a young gun, real smart; and Tova O'Brien. From the get-go, Tova had so much talent and drive, and I knew early on she'd go all the way and be one of the best political journalists ever. Tova had a gift: it was almost like she had X-ray vision capable of seeing straight through politicians' bullshit.

I told Brook and Tova: 'It's about to get real now — everyone is going to be watching us.' I was conscious that I was nowhere near Duncan's level yet. People were waiting for me to make mistakes, for our team to fail. Both Tova and Brook just nodded. They were fucking ready. We became the best team; they really had my back when I needed it most, and I'll always be thankful for that.

Quickly, I was into the grind of being Pol Ed. You had to have eyes in the back of your head and be super-alert to every movement of the politicians and your opponents. There were set pieces like Cabinet on a Monday, caucus on a Tuesday, and the 'bridge runs' — where government MPs on their way to the House came across the bridge that links the Beehive to Parliament. Reporters would talk to them on the black and white tiles. It was an opportunity to ask questions, and listen to what everyone else was up to. If you had a story you didn't want anyone else to know about, you snuck across to the other side of the bridge, to what we called the 'secret spot'. If you saw TVNZ there, it would put a huge fright up you. Were you about to be scooped? At any time of the day or night, things could break or you'd get a tip-off. I always answered my phone, no matter the time. It was ten o'clock on a Monday night and my phone was ringing? There was no 'nah, I'm finished for the day'. I answered it.

As political editor, people often wanted my ear. Even the Prime Minister. About ten to six, I'd be in position waiting to do a live cross at the top of the six o'clock bulletin, going through my final preparations. Quite often the phone rang right then — and it was John Key. I was busy and I didn't want to answer, but I couldn't afford not to because it was the prime minister. What if he wanted to give me an update? What if he had a little nugget of info? More often than not, though, he'd just be wanting to put in his two cents' worth, a last-minute bit of spin on the big story of the day before I went live. He did the same thing to Corin Dann, who had taken over as political editor at TVNZ.

Key pulled the same trick before set-piece interviews, too. You'd be about to start, getting your head in order, thinking through what questions to ask, and he'd sit down and start yapping away and distracting you with a bit of a gossip. It was hard to resist, because you didn't want to miss out, but I reckon it was actually a tactic to try to stop you from zoning in.

Political editors really became the focus of the politicians' attention any time you had a poll out. They were dying to know what was in it, to get ready to dissect it. After one poll, I was listening to Mike Hosking on Newstalk ZB because he was due to interview Key. It was the early days of streaming radio and I had tuned in via my office computer. They were on an ad break, and I suddenly realised I could hear Key and Hosking talking during the break — and they were talking about the poll and my coverage. Holy shit! Hosking was saying I was a bit of a character; he was being quite nice. But Key said, 'He's out to get me.' *Did he just say that?* Of course I wasn't out to get him. Like any other politician, he'd face strong reporting, but I wasn't out to get people for no reason. I scrambled, trying to figure out how I could rewind what I'd just heard and record it because I was thinking, *Fuck! This is extraordinary — the PM thinks I'm out to get him.*

All of a sudden, I looked up and there was Michael Fox, Key's press secretary, in the doorway. He'd sprinted down from the ninth floor of the Beehive to the *3News* office. Fox looked at me, I looked at him; no words were exchanged but he knew I'd heard it. I wasn't able to record it, and Fox got onto ZB and found there were only a handful of people streaming at the time, but yep, one of them was me. Key was soon on the blower to apologise, which was no doubt more of a clarification than an apology, and of course I accepted his word. I also told him I wasn't out to get him, and asked if he'd stop telling people I was. I wasn't too worried — it was just another morning's work in the bubble, this bizarre world.

There were often moments I'd find myself thinking, *This is so, so weird.* You'd get called up to meetings in ministers' offices — sometimes you weren't sure why. That used to happen with Gerry Brownlee, one of the senior government ministers. I liked Brownlee, he was a very funny guy. But we always used to say that he lived in 'The Sovereign State of the Seventh Floor', a bit of a la-

la land. The Prime Minister was on the ninth floor of the Beehive, the leader's staff on the eighth, and the really senior ministers were on the seventh.

Brownlee would call me up to his office and spout these sometimes crazy views on different things, or he'd want to complain. One time, he was grizzling about our coverage of something. It was a semi-serious meeting, but we were also demolishing a bottle of wine. The TV in the corner was playing music videos and it was quite distracting. He must have been relaxed because he had his tie flipped up over his shoulder. In his shirt pocket he had two phones — an official one and his personal one.

The music videos blared on, and Brownlee offered up various views on politics and the media, getting right down to a very detailed analysis of his dislike of the colours used in the *Newshub* studio.

Just another night in the Sovereign State of the Seventh Floor, and just another evening's work in the bubble.

”

I was becoming known as a bit of a character and was literally only one hand movement away from becoming a meme at any time. During a live cross on the morning show I was talking about how something would be all good and gave the 'hang loose' sign with both hands, the Hawaiian 'shaka'. Or at least that's what I meant to do. I didn't realise the way I did it had another popular meaning in New Zealand, usually accompanied by people making barking noises — the Mongrel Mob sign. The clip went viral and I earned the nickname 'Pat Dogg'. There was even a Facebook page calling for 'Paddy for PM' that earned a bit of traction.

In 2013 I got asked to be on a charity debate team in veteran Labour MP Annette King's Rongotai electorate. It was a big night on the Wellington left's social political calendar and her seat was one of the staunchest Labour strongholds in the country. The party was still going through a leadership meltdown and I'd been so busy reporting on its latest iteration that I didn't have time to prepare anything, so when I stood to speak the only things that came into my head were jokes about Labour. It did not go down well. The crowd — probably the most hardened Wellington lefties you could come across — just stared at me. Not a single line I said landed. No one was amused. Except the person next to me, in my own debating team — it was Winston Peters. I sat down and he said, 'Paddy, Paddy, Paddy — what did you do that for?' He shook his head and chuckled. 'Read the room!' Peters loved to lecture the media — this time he was bang on. I knew the next time I ever did anything like that to have a whole lot of National jokes, and vice versa.

The night eventually wrapped up, and as I was leaving Peters said, 'Want to share a taxi?' We were on our way back to town and Peters said, 'Fancy a drink?' Next minute, we headed to Courtenay Place. Although I'd reported on him a lot, I was still getting to know Peters and this was a good chance to have a yarn, away from minders and the pressures of Parliament. We ended up having a massive night out. We got to talking about why he kept coming back, why he didn't just head to the beach for good. What was it all for? I was blind drunk, but I remembered something he said and I thought it was very insightful: 'I enjoy it.' That was it — those three words. That was why he kept coming back to Parliament. He enjoyed it. I often think of that when people ask me about Peters and what makes him tick.

We zigzagged around the bars at the bottom of Courtenay Place for quite a while, and then the next morning I had to go to work and staggered into Parliament absolutely munted. Of course, there was Peters, sitting in its cafe, Copperfield's, tucking into a big breakfast and looking like he hadn't drunk a drop of alcohol. He just gave me that amazing grin, then barely acknowledged me, like the previous night had never happened. I'd look back on our night out as the midpoint of our drinking relationship — there was the incident in the Chinese takeaway when I was a student (which I dared not mention to him); this whopping night; and then a third hell of a night that would be really bad for me. But we'll get to that.

10. ABSOLUTELY BRUTAL

The Press Gallery gets its name from where the media observes Parliament. Just as there is a public gallery where punters watch the politicians in the House, there is the press gallery, an area reserved for the journos to look down into the debating chamber. If you stumble across Parliament TV, or you don't really follow politics, you may think, *What the fuck is going on there?* But if you know what to look for, it is bloody intriguing, its own world with its own language.

The first day I went into the House for Question Time — where Opposition MPs get the chance to ask questions of government ministers — John Armstrong, the doyen of the *Herald*, tugged on my sleeve and stopped me.

He was quite hard to hear because of his condition, so I leaned in to him and he said: 'People say that what happens in here doesn't matter. It does. Everything you need to know about politics you can see here if you look closely.'

And he was right. I learnt how to spot ministers who really knew their portfolios and were committed to them — and the ones who were not really into it and were wobbly on their policy. I could tell when MPs had each other's backs, and when someone was being ostracised, or was weak. I learnt how to pick up the tiniest, most subtle changes in a minister's language about a policy. It was what was said and what wasn't said, it was the body language — everything just added up, if you watched closely enough. It was like piecing a puzzle together.

It was part of the game of covering politics — a game that involved meaningful change, mingled with meaningless scandal. Looking back, there were stories I did where it all just seemed so . . . pointless. Then there were stories where important changes came about because of the pressure that built on an unpopular or bad policy.

I loved a good, old-fashioned government U-turn. Some of them were piffling, others were significant. Take National's backdown over increasing class sizes in 2012. The government was intent on pushing it through, but the pressure built, in the House, in the media, and in the public — and finally ministers backed away. That was a win for schools, for kids. I probably didn't properly appreciate it, though, because I was off hunting my next U-turn, rather than looking at the big picture.

I just want to add a disclaimer here: some of the ways I reported may sound mercenary but I'm not apologising for that. Parliament was a kill-or-be-killed environment, and I needed to be tough on politicians or they would walk all over me and, by extension, the public. I was keeping the bastards honest.

I was always hunting for a decent scalp. A scalp meant taking someone out, like a dodgy minister. Now I know that doesn't sound great, but it's what I was thinking at the time, even though I might not have acknowledged it to myself. A scalp was way above a U-turn. There was one thing above both of those for me, a coup. Covering a coup was the ultimate buzz.

David Shearer just happened to be Labour's leader right as I was at my most thirsty for scalps and coups. Ironically, while some in Labour were trying to oust Shearer, I gleaned from Key that he saw him as a threat. Shearer had a good CV, having come from the United Nations, with a background as an aid worker, and being named as the *Herald*'s New Zealander of the Year before entering Parliament. The unfortunate thing for him was he couldn't communicate well through the media, and he was a political novice.

Still, Key was scared of him getting a foothold, so he was always hyper-sensitive to coverage of Shearer. Throughout his leadership, Key was hammered over a number of stories to do with his assets, mainly about shares he owned and whether they constituted a conflict of interest. I'd even broken one myself about his blind trust, raising questions about whether it was actually blind. Then, it emerged Shearer had some money in a US bank account where he got his UN pay but he hadn't properly declared it in the MPs' Pecuniary Interests Register — he said he'd forgotten about it.

The story came out, and I didn't cover it — I was absolutely knackered on the day and my radar was a little off. My phone rang. It was Key. I couldn't believe the way he was speaking. He was tearing shreds off me and the phone was going National Party blue from the language. Key was accusing me of letting Shearer off the hook when I'd pummelled Key over his assets. To be fair, Key had a point. I should have been eviscerating Shearer, and I was scolding myself, too. But it was a real insight into Key's acute political antenna. Key knew Shearer appealed to the centre voter, and it wouldn't take much for Labour, the Greens and Winston Peters to work together and they'd be in.

Sadly for Shearer, though, his own party didn't value him. I was getting leaks from MPs all the time, even some in his camp. I got tipped off that the caucus had set him a spring deadline to improve in the polls or he'd get rolled, which I called the 'Spring Offensive'. It was absolutely brutal. And I reported every bit of brutality in a brutal way. In the middle of it all, I bumped into Shearer's wife, Anuschka Meyer, who had also worked for the UN, in human rights, and was no doubt a genuinely good human being. She didn't say anything but gave me a look of disdain. Rightfully so — I was making Shearer's life hell. I sensed she hated me. And this was from a literal humanitarian who probably couldn't hate anyone.

Still, I didn't flinch. Shearer's deadline arrived and the Spring Offensive was on, so he resigned before he was rolled, saying he didn't have the confidence of the caucus. He fronted the media and answered all the questions. He must have felt free. As he walked out of Parliament, I was waiting for him with a camera. When he opened the door and saw me, his face dropped. We locked eyes and I remember he went 'arrgh'. He'd resigned, he was going home, having rid himself of this burden — and then he was confronted by Paddy again for one last pointless jab. Poor bastard, I actually felt embarrassed for myself, like I'd gone too far, but still I asked him more questions. It didn't feel great, to be honest.

National had its own meltdowns, too. I was in an ongoing battle with them over Judith Collins. One involved an alleged conflict of interest in relation to Oravida, a company with connections to her husband. The scandal was still brewing when Key led a trade mission to Shanghai, and I was going hard on it. During a morning when there were no official duties, I tracked down the Oravida office. I couldn't believe it, but when I knocked on the door, they let me in and I wandered around with my camera filming inside. They even gave me a cup of tea. In the staffroom, I found a photograph of Key playing golf with the owner that nobody had seen before. Key hated his trade trips getting derailed, and I loved putting a rock on the tracks.

But I'll say this about Key: in 2014, he played a blinder. He could see that a majority of the public did not really understand — or care about — the scandals that dominated coverage of the campaign: conspiracies pushed by Kim Dotcom, Nicky Hager's *Dirty Politics* book, and the Collins sideshow. He just stayed above it all. The guy could take shit for weeks or even months — his resilience was astonishing. Of all the things that get written about him and why he was a good politician — often his likeability and marketability — people sometimes overlook that he was a political streetfighter who really knew how to win a scrap.

”

In every political year, there were several set pieces where the gallery actually got out of the bubble. One of my favourites was

Waitangi Day, in February. I ended up going about ten times. The *3News/Newshub* coverage was always produced by the legendary Keith Slater, who loved nothing more than a scoop.

One year when I was flying to Kerikeri, I happened to be sitting next to lawyer Donna Hall. She tipped me off to a big story — a Waitangi Tribunal claim was coming over the partial privatisation of State-owned enterprises and water rights. I was ushered into a hotel room at the Copthorne Hotel with Titewhai Harawira and Sir Graham Latimer, and handed the claim that was about to be filed. It was a massive yarn that came to dominate the political agenda — Māori uniting against the government's key policy — and here we were breaking it at Waitangi. I held the claim in my hand during my live cross, and Keith was bloody stoked. We celebrated by demolishing a few cold Steinies. I saw quite a bit at Waitangi, including being the closest to Steven Joyce's cheek when it got hit by that giant dildo in 2016 (I will never forget the 'thwack' of rubber on skin).

Through going to Waitangi, and covering the Māori Party over the years, I got an education in Māoridom. It was an awakening. One of the first times I ever went to a marae was for a Māori Party event — I had so little cultural knowledge, I didn't even know what to do with my shoes. Over the years, I've been fortunate to go to marae up and down the motu and interview many rangatira. I was really grateful — even if sometimes that meant I was put in my place.

One time I was interviewing Pita Sharples (later Sir), the educationalist and co-leader of the Māori Party. He had an idea about rehabilitation of prisoners, and I was ripping into him about it, saying it sounded as if prisoners were going flatting together. He just stopped and looked at me, and said, 'You just don't get it. This is a waste of time.' You know that feeling when your parents say they're not angry, they're just disappointed? It felt like that. I was embarrassed and it was one of those moments that made me reflect on the way I was reporting on politics. Did I really need to be an attack dog all the time?

"

In times when I was unsure of myself, or doubting things, I often sought the counsel of Gordon McBride, the old-school newsman who'd had my back when I'd started on TV. He was always keen for a chat — and a drink. One Tuesday we'd had a big night, and we were making our way home along the bottom of Courtenay Place. Gordon started wobbling like a marble statue that had come loose from its plinth. I was trying to keep him upright but he completely lost his balance, landed on top of me and conked out. I felt the full force of him on top of me and I couldn't get him off me. Two passers-by saw us and I called for help.

They looked down at me and one said, 'Paddy Gower? Is that you?'

'Yep.'

One of them got his phone out and took a selfie, which was of me and Gordon on the ground and the two of them leaning in. Priceless. Eventually, they got him off me and we bundled him into a taxi so I could get him home.

Gordon's wife, Patricia Herbert, was out playing bridge and, as luck would have it, I knew a lot about that card game — Mum had played it religiously and always got home not long after

10 p.m. I looked at my watch and it was just after ten, so I knew I had to move fast if I wanted to make sure Patricia didn't see him in this condition on a weeknight. The taxi pulled up outside their place, but being Wellington there was a decent flight of stairs up to the house.

Fear kicked in, that not only would Gordon get caught, but so would I, and I pulled him up the stairs in no time. The front door was locked but I knew the spare key was under a brick somewhere, so I frantically searched for it, making a hell of a mess in the process, but figuring Gordon could fix it the next day as penance. I found the key, got him inside, dumped him on the bed, and headed for the door. I scarpered onto the street and saw headlights coming — Patricia. I jumped into a neighbour's garden and hid, waiting for her to pass, leaving Gordon to deal with the ramifications — but they were a lot less than if she'd had to come down and scrape him off Courtenay Place.

I put the drinking down to stress relief — it was just go, go, go. I went on one of Key's trips to Washington, which came with huge pressure not to blow it. At one event, Key pulled off a coup for the small press pack travelling with him, but we completely botched it. He was speaking with US Secretary of State John Kerry at a function. We were all being kept off to the side, away from the politicians, but Key did us one hell of a solid and brought Kerry over to us — except we had no idea this was happening. Suddenly, there was Kerry in front of us, one of the most powerful people in the world, and we were completely unprepared. None of us knew what to say, so none of us said a word. Kerry awkwardly said hello, paused, and then turned. TVNZ's Corin Dann and I put our heads in our hands. 'What the fuck just happened?' The episode became known as 'The Washington Choke'.

The biggest moment of the trip was still to come and there was no way we were messing this one up. Key was going to visit President Barack Obama. I gave myself a pep talk after the Kerry incident — there were to be no more chokes under any circumstances.

To get into the room where the photo opportunity with Key and Obama was to take place at the White House, we had to line up on a veranda. It was a really hot day but I had to stay focused. Finally, the doors opened and we had seconds to get the best position. For me, that meant diving forwards, to get as close as I could to Key and Obama holding a boom mic — a microphone on a telescopic pole — to record their manufactured small talk. We were all tightly packed in like a rugby scrum. I secured a position by lying over the arm of a couch. Key was sitting in an armchair wearing the shit-eating grin to end all shit-eating grins. In the official White House photo I was splayed along the side of a couch with a shit-eating grin of my own. I even managed to get in a question about Iraq, shouting as Obama left the room. He looked down at this sweaty Kiwi, and gave a polite but bemused answer with a bamboozled look on his face.

I'd get up to all kinds of crazy antics on Key's trips. One of my early trips was to India, where I caused a diplomatic incident after a visit to the Taj Mahal. *3News* camera operator Matt Smith was with me, and in those days we had to cut a story in the field — the internet wasn't fast enough to send all your raw footage back to an editor in the newsroom. So it put a lot of pressure on the camera op and the reporter, especially with busy schedules and time differences. An FTD — Failed To Deliver — on an overseas assignment was to be avoided at all costs.

After a photo op at the Taj Mahal, Key stopped at a palace next door, and Matt and I decided there was enough time to put the story together and file before the PM's motorcade left. However, I wasn't as fast as I should've been. By the time we were ready to file, it was going to take 36 minutes to send the story, but the motorcade was leaving in ten minutes. The PM was heading to the airport to fly to the next destination in India, so it was critical we were on it. The problem was once you started sending a story, there was no sending half now and the rest later — you had to send it in one go.

The PM's staff started giving me the hurry-along. I pleaded with them: 'Can we delay the motorcade?' They asked the Indian officials but the answer was no. The PM's bodyguards from the Diplomatic Protection Service (DPS) loomed and I was arguing that maybe we could stay behind and find another way to get to the airport. They told me: 'The whole city of Agra is shut down for the motorcade to go through. Once the motorcade is through, the traffic will swarm the city again and there's no way you'll get to the airport on time. It's over, Paddy.' I was optimistic, I always believe in the possible, and was thinking, *It isn't over till it's over.* There was pressure to literally pull the plug out of the wall, and officials started to swarm, Indians looking pissed off, New Zealanders looking panicked. But there was confusion because no one from New Zealand could actually force us to get in the van. I told them, 'We're staying.'

It was a stand-off. A DPS guy said, 'That's fucking stupid, Paddy.' They all left, and it was just me and Matt wondering what the hell we were going to do.

Finally, it was uploaded. We ripped the plug out, grabbed our gear and headed for the door, without a plan of how we were going to navigate this packed city. All I knew was we were in a palace and there were no New Zealand officials around to help. The few Indian officials still in the hallways ushered us out. We burst out the palace's front doors and saw a vast roundabout and concourse before us — and guess what was there? The motorcade. Everything had been delayed and the whole line of vehicles had moved down the concourse but hadn't actually left the palace. The front cars with Key and other dignitaries on board were nudging out onto the road but the press minivan was right at the back.

Matt and I looked at each other and we knew the sprint was on. Dashing as fast as we could, lugging our bags, the tripod — everything, like a couple of madmen. The press van was starting to creep faster just as we reached it. We pounded on the back of it, the doors opened, and we were yanked inside. We'd made it. Yep, 'Paddy Luck' — the uncanny ability I seem to have to get out of a sticky situation more often than not — had come to the rescue. One of the DPS guys later ripped into me, saying I'd embarrassed the whole delegation. I felt like saying 'at least we didn't FTD', but decided it was best to shut up.

Of course there was a drink to celebrate the trip, and I ended up out late with one of the more junior reporters in the press pack. I led him astray, got very pissed, and he took a leak where he shouldn't have been and got briefly detained on the street by a police officer. We managed to talk our way out of it, but it was a very sticky situation for a while and could have gone horribly wrong.

The whole trip demonstrated the way I was operating.

Reckless. No fear. Take no prisoners. Always on attack mode and out to win. Absolutely brutal. It was brutal on me, too, though.

There were signs my judgement was fraying — I started ripping into people, good people. Yelling and losing the plot. Once, when a phone call on the work landline didn't go my way, I took the handset and hammered the main body of the phone to pieces, then did the same to the handset by smashing it on the desk. And my health was suffering, too. I couldn't sleep, my skin was dry and peeling, and I constantly had ear and eye infections.

I went to see my doctor to get sleeping pills and she said: 'One day you'll have to think about giving up this job.' I didn't say anything, but I thought, *You're talking shit. I'm not giving up this job, there's nothing wrong with me — just give me the sleeping pills.* Another time, when I was seeing her about chronic burning indigestion, she said: 'If you really want this to stop, you need to give up drinking.' Again, I thought: *Whatever. Just do your job and give me the pills to stop this burning.*

Two times, she said things to me I thought were absolutely crazy. Two times she was absolutely right. Two times I was absolutely not ready to listen. Not to my doctor, not to anyone.

11. THE PASSPORT

It's impossible to discuss TV3 without talking about the Mark Weldon era. And it's impossible to discuss the Weldon era without comparing it to a warzone. Everyone was on edge, in all corners of the business. We were working in a climate of fear, as things were so unpredictable. A former Olympic swimmer and later a top business guy, Weldon walked through the doors of TV3's Auckland office in Flower Street in August 2014 with no media experience but with a mandate to shake things up. He certainly achieved that.

I sensed Weldon did not particularly like me — I felt he thought I was anti-John Key, who he was close to. So there was a lot of pressure. I felt there was a target on my back and he was just waiting for me to fuck up. And right in the middle of all this, in October 2015, with Weldon rarking up the newsroom, I fucked up big time, putting my boss, Mark Jennings, in an awkward position when he did not need it.

The whole palaver was to do with a real warzone and began with a phone call from the Prime Minister's office. 'Can you come to a secret briefing?' All the political editors of the main news organisations gathered at Defence Force headquarters, and were told: 'We're going to take you into our confidence: the Prime Minister is going to Iraq.' Kiwi troops were based in Taji, north of Baghdad, training forces to fight in the war against the ISIS terrorists. Key had promised that if he sent troops to Iraq, he would visit them, even though it was one of the most hostile places on earth.

Now the trip was on, and he was going to take a small media contingent, including me. It had to be kept secret because of the security risk — it was believed that if ISIS knew he was going, they could plan an attack to create global headlines. Over the next few weeks, with tension building, there were more top-secret briefings at Defence HQ and logistics were sorted. Part of that was media horse-trading. Corin Dann, TVNZ's political editor, and I had to share a camera between us because there wasn't room for two — it's called a pool camera. Cam Williams, a top operator who worked for TVNZ but had previously worked at *3News* and helped me chase Chris Carter, got the call-up.

Also, between all the journalists, we had to agree on an embargo — a time when the news blackout would lift once it was safe and we could all report at the same time that Key had been to Iraq. Getting a bunch of political journalists to agree on this was probably harder than doing a peace deal with ISIS, but somehow we got there. Eventually, we were good to go. Even with the talk of danger, unlike my trip to Afghanistan as a *Herald* reporter, this time I couldn't wait. However, there was enormous pressure on me to deliver this story — not only was Key going into a warzone, but there was also much at stake in the way of New Zealand–US relations. And it all had to be done in secret. Jennings had my back, but he made it clear there was a lot on the line. The newsroom needed to give Weldon no excuse whatsoever to come at us.

”

By now, I'd done so much travel that getting around overseas was second nature. I had a drill: keeping my passport and credit card on me at all times, the rationale being even if I lost everything else, I'd be able to get by. We landed in Dubai where we were to stay before heading on to Iraq. Key was in a six-star hotel and we were in a four-star one within the same complex — it was the flashest place I've stayed in. A gigantic, sprawling place with a gigantic pool.

There was nothing to do but relax — the days ahead were going to be extremely tense. So a few of us headed to the pool. We were sitting around chewing the fat when Jane Patterson, the Radio New Zealand political editor, said, 'The only thing that could go wrong now is if we lose our passports.' Everyone kinda shrugged, and then we carried on relaxing. But her comment must have lodged in my brain because I did something I've never done before. Back in my room before we went to a beach club — did I say this place was flash and that we had time on our hands? — I thought, *Janie is right. What if I lose my passport?* So I put my passport in the hotel-room safe, and shut the door. I even read the instructions and set a pin. 'Click' went the safe door. *There — sorted.* There was no chance my passport would get stolen. If my imagined Paddy passport thieves managed to break into my room on the twenty-fourth floor, they'd be foiled by the safe.

At the beach, I went for a dip with Newstalk ZB's political editor Barry Soper. We were horsing around on the sand like a couple of bloody football stars. Life was great. That night, I went through my last-minute checks, packing and re-packing the small bag I could take with me. *I'll put my pen there. Notebook can go in there. What about spare pens — okay, there.* Over and over. I was prepared for everything, I was pumped, I was focused, I was operating at a high level.

The next morning, it was down to the lobby early, and we all piled into a minivan to go to a military base about half an hour's drive away, where an air-force plane would take us to Iraq. No one said much on the way there; we were all nervous. At the base, though there were planes on the runway, they were military planes, and the situation didn't have any airport vibes at all. The officer in charge of the elite SAS troops who would be guarding the PM and us, a guy called Jim, gave a briefing. It was next-level stuff, and I remember Jim giving me a look and seeming kind of familiar but I didn't think much of it at the time, there was so much going on. After that we had to hand in our phones — we couldn't take them to Iraq with us — so there was nothing to do but stand around having a cup of tea in the barracks. My nerves had disappeared, I felt ready. I was in one corner of the room, I saw Key in another, and then the SAS guy said, 'We're gonna go out to the plane now, so get your passports out to go through immigration.'

He hadn't even finished saying the word 'immigration' when I froze, then 'whoosh', my brain rewound at speed back to the moment when the safe door went 'click'. *Fuck.* I said out loud straight away, 'I've left my passport at the hotel.'

One of the senior army guys next to me said: 'You've what?'

'Left my passport at the hotel. Can we go get it?'

Everyone was staring. The army guy was, too, and I could read his face, which was saying: 'This is not going to work.' But he was a professional, so he swung into action, immediately ordering another soldier to drive me back to the hotel. I didn't have time to say anything to the other journos as they filed off towards the plane and I headed back the way we'd come, on a crazy mission to get my passport.

I stayed optimistic, believing that if we kept positive, we could achieve it, thinking, *This has to work.* That was not the attitude of the soldier assigned to drive me. He immediately pointed out the impossibility of the task. That there was no way we could make it back in time. He was very clearly thinking, *This is not going to work*; in fact he was saying it out loud. But I was in the zone. I asked if the soldier could speed up. He told me he would get a speeding ticket. I told him I would pay for the ticket. He still did not speed up. I made a panicked call to the hotel and they agreed to get my passport out of the safe to save us time — it was going to give us more of a chance. The soldier made a phone call to his boss and concluded we still could not make it.

What I didn't know at the time was that Key was being a good bastard and holding the plane as long as he could, even though the operation had been organised down to the second because he was due to meet the President of Iraq as soon as he landed. The soldier driving, however, remained Captain Negative. We pulled into the hotel and a staff member was standing on the sweeping driveway holding out my passport so we didn't have to stop — 'Thank you!' Finally, someone was on the same tempo as me! We headed back to the base. At precisely the legal speed limit.

There were some phone calls on the way, Key's plane was still on the runway, there was still a chance. But there was one last massive snag. Because this was a military base, I needed a visitor pass to enter. We all had one in the morning when we arrived in the van. But it was a one-use pass, and I'd used mine. I needed the guards to either let me through without checking, or if I was stopped, I would have to talk my way through. The soldier driving me was all too happy pointing out how unlikely either of those scenarios were. We pulled up to the gate, and they wanted to check my pass. I got out and started trying to talk my way in, but his English was not great, my Arabic was non-existent, and my escort was not exactly helping. But I drew on my last bit of optimism. *Come on, Paddy Luck*, I prayed.

Then I heard the roar of a plane. I looked up, and a Hercules with RNZAF insignia literally flew over our heads. My escort said: 'That's them.'

'I fucking know it's them!'

'Oh, well, looks like you missed it.' Thanks, Captain Obvious.

I was standing outside the base, absolutely broken, in 40-degree heat. I had fucked up, at an extraordinarily high level on the fuck-up scale. My opposition, Corin, was on the plane to Iraq with the PM and the other journos. And I was stranded in Dubai.

I immediately felt I had brought shame on the whole

newsroom. I had fucked up in a way that was going to cause Jennings problems with Weldon, and felt I had given the guy another stick with which to beat us. A car pulled up. It was a couple of officers from Key's DPS bodyguards. They weren't going to Iraq — it was the job of the SAS to protect him over there. So they asked if I wanted a lift back into town. I didn't have any other options, so I hopped in. I needed to ring Jennings, but I was in tears and was too embarrassed to make this possibly career-ending phone call in front of the DPS. Then I thought about how they were the most discreet people you'd ever know, given prime ministers make sensitive calls around them all the time. They heard all sorts of scandal and gossip and never breathed a word. I dialled Jennings.

It went straight to voicemail. There was no way I was leaving a message. I hung up. The phone rang. It was Jennings; he was at the movies, but had jumped out after seeing my call, knowing I should be on the way to Iraq. 'Hey . . . I've missed the plane . . . I left my passport at the hotel,' I said, in a state of extreme shock.

There was silence. I have to hand it to Jennings, he kept calm. Then he asked where Cam was, the pool camera. 'He's on the plane.'

'Well, I guess you're just going to have to wait for him to get back and make a story based on the footage he gets.' He must have been spewing, and this was a major fuck-up by one of his most senior journos. But somehow he didn't lose his rag — to me anyway. I hate to think what he said when he hung up the phone.

”

The DPS dropped me back at the hotel and I spent a few hours figuring out if there was any other way to get there, but it was a lost cause. Someone from the army came to see me and said they'd tried as well, even asking the Americans, but came up short. There was absolutely nothing to do, but wait 36 hours until they got back. I wallowed around Dubai in a state of shock. I didn't even feel like drinking and I certainly didn't feel like sleeping. I tried to take in some of the hotel's luxury with some pool time and was wandering around the massive hotel complex in the early hours of the morning. On the way through the lobby, I chatted to the reception desk. I said something about how I was supposed to be with the PM, and the woman said, 'Oh, yes, he's back in the hotel tonight.'

If anybody knew what time they were coming back, it would be me, and he was definitely going to be away, so I said, 'Tomorrow night.'

But she said, 'No, tonight.' Strange, but I figured she'd just got mixed up, so didn't say anything and went back to my room.

I managed to get a bit of sleep when my phone rang. It was the PM's press secretary, Michael Fox. I was seriously confused. 'Foxy? Hello?'

'You are the luckiest bastard I know. We're back in Dubai and we're thirty minutes away from the hotel.' They'd got as far as Baghdad but a sandstorm had prevented them from flying to the military camp at Taji, so they'd spent hours on the runway waiting and eventually decided to return to Dubai and try again the next day. The journos hadn't even got out of the plane.

Have you ever seen the footage of All Black Ali Williams immediately after New Zealand won the 2011 Rugby World Cup?

He let out an enormous cheer and bear-hugged John Campbell. It was pure joy writ large. That was me. I jumped out of bed and stood there in my gruts and roared a primaeval sound: 'Yesssssss!!!'

I headed downstairs and arrived as the minivan with all my journo mates turned up. They looked like crap, and were tired, hungry and frustrated. It was quite the turnaround. They'd been holed up on the plane, while I'd been poolside. Barry Soper was particularly grumpy about it. 'Fuck you, Paddy. Fuck you.' I laughed. I love Bazza.

The trip was back on the next morning, Jennings was a happy man, and the embargo meant news of my fuck-up was on the down low. Passport in hand, it was all go and all the hardcore SAS guys had a good laugh when I jumped on the plane. Their boss, Jim, gave me a nice firm handshake and seemed particularly happy. As the plane took off I said over the roar of the engines, 'I am back, I am fucking back!'

”

I was wandering around Camp Taji that night and started having small talk with SAS Jim when he said, 'You don't remember me, do you, Paddy?' I knew he was the guy who'd briefed us back in Dubai and looked at me sideways. I kind of felt I did know him but with all the stress I admitted I couldn't place him. 'I'm James,' he said — the son of Keith, one of my Old Man's best mates who'd died of cancer not long after we found out about Mum's diagnosis; the guy I saw at his dad's funeral, shouldering all that responsibility for his family. 'You're fucking joking! I'm so sorry, mate!' After growing up together in New Plymouth, going to barbecues at each other's houses, here we were both in Iraq, but talk about polar opposites — one of us was a highly capable SAS officer, the other a journalist who couldn't even remember to bring his passport.

Our troubles weren't over, either. The Iraqi government tweeted that Key was in the country — while we were still in a news blackout and stuck in Iraq. Then another sandstorm hit, trapping us at Camp Taji. The Americans sent a couple of Chinook helicopters to get Key out, and Cam and I ended up in the back of the second one with some of the SAS. There were insane scenes as we powered through the sandstorm with Apache attack helicopters flying as an escort. The Paddy-in-Iraq comedy show continued, with Cam and I having a loud argument about who would take a photo, which would be epic but against the rules. An SAS trooper interrupted us by growling, 'Just take the fucking photo.' Cam took the shot.

The helicopters landed, and the SAS were swearing again — we were back at Camp Taji, the sandstorm had turned us back. Things were getting a little intense. We ended up running onto the runway and getting back on the New Zealand Air Force plane, which seized a break in the sandstorm. Its anti-aircraft flares were triggered as we took off, and now, after about 72 hours of this crazy mission, I started to lose my mind. But we were soon back in Dubai and got the story out. I remember the live cross to the studio coming on for pre-show checks, and it was Sam Hayes, saying, 'Paddy, it sounds like you've been having an interesting time.'

'I've certainly learnt some new life skills,' I said.

”

I never heard if Weldon found out about my lost passport. I'm sure he would've said something if he had as there were a few other occasions when he rang me directly — it was highly unusual for the CEO of the company to call the political editor. There was the time after 'This is the Fucking News' when he wanted to know how to monetise that viral clip, which was harmless enough.

But there were a couple of other times when he got in touch that I didn't feel comfortable with at all. He had well-known affiliations with John Key and National, having run a huge job summit for Key. Not long after the 2015 Budget, Weldon wanted to catch up with me in Wellington. I met him and he gave me what I took as a veiled critique of the coverage. He said 'someone in politics, not John' had pointed out how the Budget's main angle was Bill English raising benefits and I'd run that story second, when it should have led the bulletin. And then there was a figure that was wrong. I remember thinking, *These are bloody specific things for a CEO to be talking to a political editor about.* But I didn't push back, I didn't have the confidence. It was just really off-putting.

Another time came when Jacinda Ardern wrote a column about him in the *Sunday Star-Times*. It was an open letter to Weldon about how, in her opinion, he'd wrecked TV3. I got a phone call from Weldon, asking me if I'd read the column.

'Oh, sort of skimmed it, yeah.' Of course, I'd read every single word of it — about five times.

My recollection is that he wasn't happy and he was getting some advice. He wanted to push back against Ardern and was keen to know what I thought of that. I was racking my brain, thinking, *What is going on here?*

But I didn't want to say a word. Because the only thought I had was that as political editor I sure as fuck didn't want to be dragged into it — I didn't want to be in the middle of a scrap between a rising politician and the boss of my company. But I couldn't exactly say any of that.

I stalled for time and said I'd have a think about it. He said he'd ring me back soon. I immediately headed outside for fresh air and thought, *Shit, what just happened?* I didn't feel I could ring my direct bosses because it was just such a chaotic time. What was I going to do?

I was dreading his next phone call. I needed a way out of this — and one came along, very unexpectedly. 'Paddy Luck' struck again — Weldon resigned, saving me from ever having to answer his awkward questions.

12.
TAKING ON THE DONALD

Bizarrely, just before Mark Weldon left, his era of chaos gave me the chance to meet Donald Trump. It was 2016, and Trump was starting his political rise before Super Tuesday, a crunch point for the presidential wannabes, make or break, and I really wanted to go. Problem was, it was right at the time that Weldon was putting the pressure on TV3, with everyone going batshit crazy at work, and heaps of cost-saving measures being put in place — for example, all printing had to be done in black and white and double-sided. I figured with all the cost-cutting I had almost zero chance.

Mark Jennings was in Wellington and I thought, *I'm just going to pitch it to him — what have I got to lose?* It was only a few days out from a Republican debate in Houston and there was a direct flight from Auckland, so I went armed to the meeting with the costs. Sitting down with Jennings, I started my big pitch that I'd memorised. I'd only just started when this strange smile appeared on his face and he said, 'Yep, sounds good, off you go.' I was stunned. *Huh?* I hadn't even got to the good bits. I didn't understand what had happened, but there was no way I was going to argue, so next thing I was at the airport with Matt Smith on camera.

We were waiting for the flight when, ping, an email arrived. 'Mark Jennings has resigned . . .' It was classic Jennings. He obviously knew he was going to pull the pin and had snuck through this half-pitched idea on the way out. In the back of my mind I was thinking I'd get called back as soon as we landed in Houston, but it was too late to worry about that — we were on the runway. The call never came; with so much going on at TV3 no one was worrying about me when the place was in meltdown.

Because we'd scrambled in a rush, Matt and I hadn't applied for 'credentials', which you needed to get into the big events like the Republican debate in Houston, held at a gigantic campus at the University of Texas. We rocked up anyway, pleaded our case and were told they might be able to get us in once the debate opened and they could tell who hadn't shown up. With six hours until doors opened and nowhere else to be, we figured we might as well just sleep on the grass in the university grounds under a nearby tree. This at least showed we were serious, and they let us into the 'media room' — a gymnasium with thousands of journalists and hundreds of TVs showing the debate, which was going on in an even bigger gymnasium next door. I was beginning to understand how huge American politics was.

There was a 'mix zone' where prominent political leaders and pundits who'd been at the debate would wander through afterwards and talk to the media, and there were stalls with the main TV networks scattered around, going live the whole time. Word got round that Trump might come in and give the media a 'spray' in the mix zone. So we squeezed against a barrier fence; I was just stoked to be there — the thought of getting Trump on camera or even getting a soundbite was an extra buzz.

We watched the debate and Trump did well. But would he emerge? One of the biggest figures on the Republican political scene, Texas Governor Greg Abbott, sauntered through and came straight over towards us. He talked to a short Texan guy next to me who'd been really helpful, giving me tips like 'use your accent, Trump might like it'. I figured he must be a big deal since Abbott sought him out, so I asked where he was from and he said, 'Breitbart.' I'd never heard of it, but within months, it was world-famous; the far-right news organisation tied up with Trump strategist Steve Bannon.

"

Next minute, Trump walked out surrounded by hangers-on, all wearing slick suits. He was 50 metres away. He went to one of the stalls for an interview with the big TV networks and then headed to the barrier fence for a spray. He kept this up, zigzagging back and forth — interview, spray, interview, spray — edging his way towards where we were. I realised we were in with a chance. We were mashed up with all these other journos. Heart racing, I checked on Matt: 'You all good?' We were pumped. I was in the ninety-ninth percentile. I was thinking, *Believe in the possible. We can get Trump.*

I was rehearsing in my head the question I wanted to ask, and visualising getting Trump. Then Trump suddenly walked our way, about a metre from us, looking straight at me. I couldn't believe it but I got my mouth to move and words came out. 'A question from New Zealand . . .'

As soon as he heard that, he knew it was a waste of his time — no votes in New Zealand — so he said: 'Say hello to Bob Charles. I love Bob Charles. You know who Bob Charles is?'

'Yes, I do — famous golfer,' I replied.

He looked down the barrel of the camera — I'd been relegated to a side role by that stage — and said: 'Your greatest golfer.'

And that was it, he was off. I didn't get to ask my question, which was about the Trans-Pacific Partnership trade deal being promoted by New Zealand but hated by Trump; I thought it might have provoked an answer.

Still, we had Trump, kind of. But not as well as I wanted. I wanted more.

"

Super Tuesday was still two days away. Matt and I took advantage of the upheaval back home — we couldn't get hold of anyone to ask permission for anything — so we gave ourselves permission to fly to the Texas city of Fort Worth for a Trump rally. It was when physical violence was first starting to break out at Trump rallies. We bumped into Jack Tame, TVNZ's US correspondent — he'd been covering the whole election, whereas we'd just parachuted in. Jack and I talked about what we were planning for Super Tuesday. Trump was going to be at Mar-a-Lago in Florida, but it was well known he never let in foreign journalists. However, Matt and I were still giving ourselves permission to travel, and had decided to go anyway. I said to Jack, 'Look, full transparency, we're going to Mar-a-Lago.'

Jack wasn't, but, being a good bastard, he gave me an email address that apparently offered the best shot at getting credentials for Mar-a-Lago. 'I've never had any luck,' he said.

I wrote an email, and sent it off without much hope. A day later, Matt and I were filming on some rocks across the water from Mar-a-Lago with a whole lot of other foreign journalists when I got a reply. We were in. I still have no idea of how or why Paddy Gower from *Newshub* was invited into Trump's press conference, but some other foreigner could have our rock.

The next day, we turned up as soon as the gates opened, about eight hours before things were kicking off, and were steered straight to the press-conference location, the appropriately named White & Gold Ballroom. I strode up to one of the front rows and used Matt's gaffer tape to fasten my briefcase to a seat so no one could shift it if I needed to go to the toilet (where even the flusher was gold). All the producers for the big networks arrived to secure places for their hosts.

Then the BBC turned up, the only other foreign media in the place, and took the seat next to me. It was Jon Sopel, the BBC's North America editor — a media superstar who'd just interviewed Barack Obama in the White House. We discussed cricket and a little bit of small talk, but we were both zoning in. I was here for a second chance to ask Trump a decent question. There was nowhere to get food; I got through the day with a bit of water and a couple of cookies. Matt checked my mic about a hundred times, and we talked things through — he'd be on the wide shot so that if I did get a question, we had it on camera.

I spent a lot of time believing in the possible again, visualising what could happen and what I would say. I was back in the ninety-ninth percentile. The whole room was psyched up, then Trump walked in, and opened it up for questions straight away. Both Jon Sopel and I desperately tried to get Trump's attention — I had my notebook folded in half like my old idol Tony Wall used to back at the *Herald*, and I waved it above my head. There was no rhyme or reason as to who Trump chose to ask a question. Suddenly, he turned over to where we were and pointed. We were both out of our seats. Sopel thought it was him, I thought it was me, and Trump was pointing down the middle. Then his finger tilted in my direction. I heard Sopel say 'Fuck' as he slumped back into his chair.

I was the only one standing in the room, Trump was looking straight at me again and I got a bolt of energy. It was the biggest stage I'd been on, the whole world was watching. I'd been rehearsing my question all day. 'Donald Trump, you've told us a lot about what kind of president you'll be for America. I want to know: what kind of president would you be for the world?' He started answering and I sat down. He was rambling away and hadn't even finished when my phone blew up with people asking, 'Was that you, PG?' The press conference was beaming live around the world to millions. Holy shit, I'd done it. I'd got The Donald.

”

A few months later, I was back in the US for the 2016 presidential election itself, Trump versus Hillary Clinton. It was day one of my coverage and things went viral. We were at a Trump rally in Miami, when I approached a guy who'd come to be known on the internet as 'Visor Guy'. He was wearing a sun visor and carrying a 'Make America Great Again' sign. He said, 'I'm not talking to the Clinton media, you guys are a sell-out.'

'I'm from New Zealand, though. I'm not part of the Clinton media.'

He seemed confused and looked around for a couple of seconds then said, 'What's Zealand?' He didn't seem to know New Zealand was a country — 20.8 million views of the video later, a lot of people had seen Visor Guy.

The day before the election, we headed to Scranton, Pennsylvania, a typical blue-collar former steel town. Then-Democratic Vice President Joe Biden famously came from there — but Trump was holding a rally, a symbolic middle-finger to the Democrats. We interviewed people in the long queue to get into the venue, and they all seemed . . . normal. There was no sign of any Visor Guy-type crazies. There was no sign of craziness at all. There were business owners. There were plenty of educated people. There were regular moms and dads. They were all normal. There was a phenomenon going on here.

Trump came out and said, 'We are just one day away from the change you have been waiting for your entire life.' And I truly felt that weight of history in the air. The polls were saying it was going to be Clinton, but I was thinking, *If there're more Scrantons out there, Trump is going to win this thing.* And the next day, The Donald became President of the United States.

”

By the time of that 2016 presidential election, I was already becoming a US political veteran.

My first taste of it was back in 2012, in that batty year when I was the political editor-in-waiting. I was seen as a maverick and there was a lot of chatter that I didn't yet have the gravitas to be political editor. When word leaked I was due to take over from Duncan Garner, there was a story in the *Herald on Sunday* and in the interview I said I was declaring war on politicians. It was a bit edgy for a political editor. Veteran gallery journo Barry Soper hit me up straight away, and said, 'Congratulations — but what's this crap you're saying? This is embarrassing.' Looking back it was a naive thing to say. It underlined what people were saying about my lack of gravitas — but it also showed my mindset at the time. I felt the older guard in the gallery and the political chattering classes were looking down their noses at me and I didn't fit in — and the more I felt that, the more I rebelled against it.

Richard Sutherland, who was the deputy head of news at TV3, came up with the idea of sending me to the States to cover the US elections to bolster up my CV and show I had what it took to step up as political editor.

I landed in Chicago and bought a copy of the *Chicago Sun-Times*. The coverage was page after page, and I freaked out, thinking, *This is too big. I can't do this.* Then a US-based Kiwi camera operator, Sam Winslade, joined me and it was exactly what I needed. He knew his way around, had a grasp of US politics, and was fizzing. Off we went and started doing offbeat stuff like going to a small town in Wisconsin and door-knocking the next-door neighbour of the Republican nominee for vice president, Paul Ryan. We got a bonkers interview and it showed me that anything was possible, with Americans such good talent on camera.

In those days, doing live crosses was expensive and a lot of hoo-ha. You had to buy a satellite slot for five minutes and be ready to go at your allotted time. Reporters from around the world would line up, preparing to step onto a small podium and speak into the camera that was set up and ready to go. One day I was due to cross live with Rachel Smalley on the morning show and I arrived a bit late. I jumped onto the podium and got straight into it. Because I'd been late, I ran over my time slot but no one stopped me so I just kept going and Rachel kept asking questions. I heard a kerfuffle beside me and next thing a guy yanked me off the podium. Turned out he was from Sweden, and he was desperate to get his slot for the evening news, so it was a fair cop and would turn out to be a good lesson.

A few nights later, election night, and I was covering Obama at the Democratic HQ in Chicago. *3News* anchor Mike McRoberts was with Mitt Romney, the Republican challenger, in Massachusetts. I didn't really know Mike at that stage, but as I stood under the bleachers getting ready to go live at the top of the six o'clock news I started to freak out. The noise was phenomenal, the pressure was mounting. I rang Mike and was straight up: 'I'm choking here, mate. I don't know if I can do this.' Another swing state fell Obama's way and there was another deafening cheer. *Shit.* It just piled on more pressure. Mike could hear my desperation. In his calm, newsreader voice that has soothed the nation in times of trouble, he said: 'It's going to be okay, mate.

Just say what's happening. You'll be fine.' I instantly felt better. Then another cheer went up. *Shit.* I instantly felt terrible again. At a few minutes to six o'clock, I was let through to the live-cross point, and I could see the whole scene for the first time: the stage, and an empty podium lit up and waiting for Obama. *Holy. Fuck. So. Many. People.*

Also there was a problem: I should have been in front of the camera already, but there was a big Spanish-speaking guy still doing his cross. I said to the person in charge of the live-cross point, some guy called Lance, 'Get him off — I've got to be on air at six.' Lance tried talking to him, but he wouldn't listen, he just kept up his live cross. *Tick, tick, tick.* Six o'clock loomed. Alright, I knew what to do here: what the Swedish guy did to me. I switched from being worried to being an out-and-out psycho. I put both hands on this reporter as he was beaming live to who-knows-what country, pulled the earpiece out of his ear, grabbed the mic out of his hands, dispatched him off the live-cross point, assumed the position and looked over to Lance, who looked pretty shocked. But he gave me a nod because he knew that was the only way the situation was going to be resolved.

Lance flicked the switch and I heard producer John Hale in the Auckland newsroom say, 'Is that you, Paddy?'

'It's me, John. Let's go.' It must have been 5.59 p.m. back at home because the next thing I heard was Hilary Barry at the top of the news. I realised I hadn't been thinking about what to say because I'd been in a physical tussle, and had gone into full streetfighter mode. Next minute Hilary asked her question, and the words just came out of my mouth: 'He's back, he's back big time.' Obama had been re-elected for another term, which

I called the 'second coming'. I'm pretty sure I wasn't showing gravitas, but it was good television.

On our last day, Sam and I wanted to see how the result was going down in middle America. I'd been surprised to see how divisive Obama was, so we headed into this little Ohio town called Camden, which was full of Joe and Jane Americans. It was snowing, which probably didn't help, but it felt bleak and grim. I'd come straight off the high of the Obama victory party, and hearing his soaring oratory; in Camden they just did not care. Not one bit. They were disillusioned with politics. All they'd talk about was the economy and how it was wrecked. As well as the snow, there was rubbish all over the ground, and abandoned old stuff everywhere. It was like they'd all just given up caring.

I left Camden thinking, *This country is seriously broken. What's wrong?* America was a lot different to what I'd thought. The politics was so polarised, it was all heat and no light. There were no options for people, just two candidates, one blue and one red. Then there were these apathetic people on Struggle Street in Camden. I felt moved by what I'd seen, a little shaken even. It was still years before Trump came on the scene, but looking back now it was in towns like Camden where Trumpism started to rise.

”

I was back in America for the 2020 election, too — my third presidential election. Over the eight years since 2012, I had covered Republican and Democratic conventions, saw rallies for Hillary Clinton, Obama, and plenty for Trump. I reported from twenty states, and I loved reporting in America, a great country with plenty of good people still chasing the American dream. But what I saw in Camden in 2012, in Scranton in 2016, and in other towns since, was not the American dream — it was the American malaise. From the distance of New Zealand it was hard to understand what had happened there, but on the ground in those places I could really see it.

That dislocation we'd seen in 2012 was now widespread — dislocation from politics, dislocation from government, dislocation from the economy, and dislocation from the mainstream media, too. Looking back, what I was reporting on wasn't just the politics of America — as exciting as that was, with all the show business around it — it was the social phenomenon that was going down. I was watching a society tearing itself apart.

In 2020, the tension was heightened because of Covid and the ferocity whipped up by the Trump versus Joe Biden duel. As I left to return to New Zealand, Biden was announced as the winner, but I just knew that wasn't going to be the end of it. I flew out fearing how far Trump would push things. Three months later, Capitol Hill was stormed.

13.
OUT IN THE MIDDLE

In the run-up to New Zealand's 2017 election, one of the big questions at *Newshub* (as *3News* had become known) was who would host the leaders debate. It was always one of the most-watched set pieces of the campaign, the leaders of Labour and National going head-to-head on live TV. TVNZ traditionally ran two debates, and *Newshub* one. John Campbell had moderated ours for years, but he was gone after *Campbell Live* got axed. It was one of the more hotly contested roles going, but I guessed Duncan Garner, who'd moved into a presenting role, or Lisa Owen, the formidable interviewer fronting the weekend politics show *The Nation*, would do it. The question came up at an election planning meeting led by Mark Jennings' replacement, Hal Crawford, a recent arrival from Australia.

'Paddy will do it,' said Hal, almost off the cuff. The room went quiet. As the outside chance, I was shocked and pretty sure he'd change his mind later, but he never did.

Lisa came to see me and said: 'I'm gutted, I wanted to do it. But the one thing that overrides that is I want to go out and beat TVNZ no matter what, so I'm going to help you.' There aren't many people in broadcasting who would have done that — suck up the disappointment and pour themselves into helping prepare the person who'd got the job instead. Plenty of people would say they'd help, but not really put in the grunt. Not Lisa. She was the ultimate team player. She became the debate coach, put in hours of research, brainstormed — and gave me the best question you could ever ask in a debate, one that threw the leaders from the get-go.

Being given the job of the leaders debate was a bit of a lifeline for me. By 2017, issues with my state of mind and the pressure of the job were coming to a head. As political editor, I was not on form. I was making missteps and blowing up at people all over the place. I did an interview with Greens co-leader James Shaw on *The Project*, a show that had a lighter tone — but I aggressively went for Shaw's jugular and everybody working on the show seemed a little shocked. I felt bad about it, and on *The AM Show* the next morning I apologised — which didn't look good either. Duncan was hosting *AM* and said to me, 'What are you doing?' My radar was off big time. Another day I had a volcanic blow-up at Andrew Campbell, the Greens' chief strategist, about something utterly meaningless. He later rang me, not to have a go, but to ask if I was okay. At that moment, I was taken aback: *Whoa, this guy is really worried about me. Maybe I should get help?* But soon after I was back at it, scrapping away again.

The debate, though, got me away from the day-to-day grind

— even if what I'd been asked to do was far beyond anything I'd done before. There was huge pressure. But I did something interesting: for the first time in my life, I gave up the booze, out of fear. I had to do everything in my power to get ready for the debate or else I knew I was going to fuck it up.

The campaign itself was frenzied. Jacinda Ardern had unexpectedly taken over from Andrew Little as Labour leader, giving the party the boost it needed. Polls showed support for the two major parties was neck and neck. On the day of the debate, National campaign mastermind Steven Joyce threw a curveball, claiming Labour's numbers had an $11 billion 'fiscal hole'. It was a typical calculated move from Joyce, who knew how to win elections and was a real hard-arse.

There was one time Joyce took exception to some of my coverage and started a fight with me over text. He wouldn't stop. Ping, ping, ping. I was at home trying to watch a cricket one-dayer and I remember wishing he would watch it, too, and stop worrying about the point he was trying to make. But the texts kept coming. I tried to enjoy the cricket, but there was no way he'd stop without having won. Then I looked on Twitter and there was a tweet from him — at the cricket. He was at the ground, saying how much he was enjoying the game. I realised what a formidable mind he had — he probably *was* enjoying the cricket, but at the same time he could run a sideline operation attacking a journalist for his coverage. So, yeah, that was Joycey.

Anyway, on the day of the debate, he tossed the fiscal-hole grenade to try to derail the debate, and Labour's campaign along with it. It was not what I needed as it was a grenade for my final prep, too, but hey, that's politics. I was in my changing room trying to memorise the questions when I realised I could hear National leader Bill English in the next room, with a locked door between us. I was tempted to press my ear against the door, but knew I shouldn't, it wouldn't be right. So I immediately pressed up against it. Then I heard one of his staff say, 'Pike River might come up' — I'd been covering the West Coast mining disaster relentlessly. English said: 'Oh, Paddy's obsessed with that.' I thought, *You betcha Pike River is going to come up.* We already had a question prepared.

I realised if I could hear them, they could hear me. Although I was on my own, I'd been practising the questions out loud, and letting off steam by waa-hooing and doing violent claps every now and then. They must have thought I was a madman. It was time to go, so I walked out and said to the crowd, 'Anyone nervous?' They all cracked up. It was great to break the ice. Then, as we went through our final checks, the earpiece fell silent. It was my line of communication with the producers and I couldn't hear a thing. I called the soundie over: 'We're in the shit here, mate — I can't hear the producer.' The earpiece was important so they could keep me in the loop, and tell me when to go to ad breaks. The soundie was desperately fiddling around with cables, pulling them out and plugging them in. Nothing. There was no time to worry anymore. We were starting.

I experienced something I never had before. A sense of calm, a sense of moving from that ninety-ninth percentile where I liked to operate, straight to a hundred. Everything dropped away. I thought to myself: *I can do this without comms. All I need to do is ask questions until someone waves and then I'll know it's time for an ad break.* And then I thought: *You're so ready, you could chuck these questions away and do it from memory.* With 90 minutes of questioning ahead that would have been incredibly difficult, if not impossible, but that's how I felt.

We began and I lobbed them the brilliant question Lisa had come up with: 'Can you survive in politics without lying?' English wobbled and rambled. Ardern just said, 'I believe it is possible to exist in politics without lying.' *Boom, here we go*, I thought. *We have a debate.* We punched right on and suddenly the comms came to life and the producer was yelling that it was time for the first ad break.

The rest of the debate was a blur. I asked a question about what they would march in the streets for and English said he'd march for himself to govern again. It was a strange answer and Ardern just gave me this little grin. Another question was about what had changed since English had lost in 2002, when he was previously National leader, and he said, 'I got back up again.' And the crowd cheered. I gave English a nod of acknowledgement and he nodded back. When it came to talking about marijuana decriminalisation, I asked what should happen to someone caught with cannabis the size of a muesli bar. For some reason, English started cracking up, with this weird giggle. I'd been watching this guy for nine years and I'd never seen him laugh this much. I realised we were all having fun.

Suddenly it was over. I looked for my Old Man, who was in the audience. It was important to have him here. And I thought about the Old Lady, too. She'd grown up in Manurewa, just down the road from the debate venue in Manukau. It was special to think of how Nana and Grandad had moved here to give their family a better life, and here I was, their grandson, moderating a debate between two people seeking the most powerful job in the country. It was a high point of my career. I'd pulled it off, I could not be any happier.

Back in the changing room, I cracked into a box of cold beers. The alcohol drought was over, thank fuck.

”

When the 2020 debate came around, I was out in the middle again — Ardern versus Judith Collins. On the team this time were experienced operators Todd Symons and Maryanne Ahern, and a brilliant young reporter called Zac Fleming. Although I had the 2017 debate under my belt, I wanted to take my skill set up a level.

I reached out to Conrad Smith, the double-World-Cup-winning All Black who'd been a couple of years behind me at Francis Douglas Memorial College and had joined us on those infamous peloton rides to school into the staunch headwind. I knew Conrad was very much into the mental side of things, and he had managed to get himself up to play in — and win — a second World Cup final. I figured that, once you eliminated the obvious differences between an All Blacks centre and a debate moderator, there were things I could learn from him. What was the psychological framework I could put around myself to ensure I reached the top of my game? I really wanted to work with the power of my mind rather than acting in an ad hoc way and finding it by accident as I'd done in the last debate, or for that matter throughout my entire career. I wanted to find some control.

Over video calls from France, Conrad shared some of the

secrets of how he prepared for test matches, of how he dealt with pressure. With the debate, like a rugby final, I knew I had one shot to nail it, and I'd be doing it in front of about a million viewers.

We talked about preparation — with the debate, that involved brainstorming, mapping out questions and then what I called 'mind-mapping' the leaders so I deeply understood their positions and could anticipate their answers. The team and I worked out what we thought the leaders were going to say. That way I could push back and constantly challenge them. I wanted to get the leaders into a free-wheeling situation, to make their brains work so fast they were thinking on their feet. That way I'd get real answers out of them, rather than learnt, rote lines.

Conrad also spoke about getting back to basics, which for him was tackling and catching and passing the ball. It made me think: *What are my basics?* I decided it was listening and reacting. I had to listen to every single word, and if there was the slightest change in their position I had to react.

Another important thing Conrad said was to be in the 'now', be in the moment, and to express myself. He talked about how he smiled as he walked onto the field before a test match, how he had learnt to enjoy the moment. In 2017 I'd been so tight and wrapped up, I didn't enjoy it. So in 2020 I decided to express myself — smile, be calm, take on the pressure, enjoy the challenge.

During the debate I had a piece of paper in front of me that read 'Listen. React. Back myself.' That was what I was here to do — I had the skills, I had to back myself to be a great broadcaster. This was all part of learning to control my mindset, something I now call 'trained optimism', forcing myself to believe in the possible, to think positively, visualising the best thing that could happen. For the debate, that meant visualising the questions going well, visualising the leaders debating, visualising the crowd reacting, controlling and using the power of my imagination to visualise the best thing happening, figuring out what it would take to get there, and then building the process required. I also reflected on how I was out in the middle on behalf of all Kiwis, and I had to do a good job for them.

I was ready. On the night itself a funny thing happened right at the start. Sam Smith, a comedian and friend, was warming up the crowd — doing a routine and making them laugh before we got underway. But he didn't hear the floor manager say it was time to stop. We were seconds from starting and he was still standing in front of me, telling jokes to the crowd. I said, 'Hey, Sam, bro — get off the stage.'

He replied, 'Oh, shit' — and those were the first two words people tuned in for the broadcast heard on TV. It proved that no matter how much preparation you did, a comedian could still mess with your shit.

"

After all the work Conrad had done with me, when he got in touch after the debate asking if I could return the favour, of course I said yes. In the All Blacks, Conrad had set up something called 'clubrooms' where a senior player organised a social night. When Conrad retired from internationals, Sam Cane took over the role. Sam wanted to organise a bit of a debate within the team. They wanted me to come along and moderate. When the All Blacks call, you answer. So, even though it was the week before the 2020 election and I was really busy, of course I said yes.

Part of the clubrooms tradition was that players wore the jerseys of their original club. I was supposed to be on *The Project* that night and had asked for the night off but the bosses weren't keen. As a compromise, they let me attend the All Blacks gig before the show, so long as I was ready to go live on air as soon as I got back. This meant I had to be in my studio make-up. Now, wearing make-up was one thing. Wearing studio make-up was quite another. It wasn't just a bit of powder on my nose — they applied industrial-scale levels of gunk to my face, fiddled around with my eyebrows, and put truckloads of product in my hair. It was full noise. So there I was — with my studio make-up, wearing a funky blue jacket that the stylist had chosen for me — on my way to meet the All Blacks.

The players started turning up in their club jerseys and flip flops, these giant men, and I looked like something out of Madame Tussauds. About 35 of them filled this big room we were in down at a waterfront hotel in Auckland. I was standing awkwardly off to the side. Luckily for me, the Barrett brothers arrived — Scott, Beauden and Jordie — and I knew them through Francis Douglas, so they came over and had a yarn.

Even before we started, you could see the competitiveness in the All Black camp. Three of them had been selected to present. They had to make a convincing argument that the cause they'd chosen was the most worthwhile. Anton Lienert-Brown, the midfield back, came up to me before the start, giving me a rundown of his topic and trying to get feedback — it was like he was trying to get the inside word from the ref before the game started. These boys were serious. Lienert-Brown's topic was to do with getting people off the dole and back into work. Another back, Damian McKenzie, had built a case around stopping people from pre-loading — getting boozed up at home before going out for the night.

The only forward was prop Joe Moody. Everybody tends to judge props and make assumptions about their intelligence. Moody was about to make a mockery of that. I snuck a peek at his notes and he'd written these really impressive points in the most beautiful handwriting. And he'd chosen a really intellectually elevated topic, too, to do with justice and reconciliation in the Catholic Church. It was very high-brow, and he presented it like a pro.

Frankly, in my opinion, he wiped the floor. I gave the debate to Moody. It did not go down well with Lienert-Brown, who immediately came over and started remonstrating with me, wanting to take it upstairs to the video ref, I suppose.

After the debate, I was asked to say a few words. They wanted some hot takes about the election, which was just a few days away, so I gave them my thoughts. Then I just started riffing a bit. They were due to play the Wallabies on Sunday, the day after the election, at Auckland's Eden Park. I said to them that they didn't need to hear from me to get motivated. Who was I? But I just asked them to think about how they were playing before a country that had been through Covid lockdowns and plenty of stress that year (and there was more to come, especially in Auckland). I said people had had so much taken away, they hadn't been able to lead normal lives, and they'd been robbed of so much joy. On Sunday, I told the players, they had the opportunity to go out and put on a game for people to enjoy.

I couldn't tell if the message got through — you never know if your words have any meaning. But they walloped the Wallabies, 27–7. Caleb Clarke was unstoppable on the wing and it was said in the official match report that he made storming runs that seemingly dragged his team along with him. He was the MVP that day.

A few years later Caleb was on *The Project*, and during the show he said he'd met me before and started talking about the clubrooms night. *Oh, here we go*, I thought. *He's going to bring something up about the make-up or an inane remark I made . . .* I braced myself. Instead, he talked about how he remembered what I'd said and how inspiring it was. I was stunned. It was a beautiful postscript.

It was also a reminder that I got to do some pretty cool shit down the years — even if sometimes it had been a terrifying ride, like when I lost all my sight in one eye.

14. GOING BLIND

Before I tell the story of going blind in one eye, I need to wind the clock back a bit, to 2014, to what I call the weirdest election campaign ever. It was my first as political editor, and there was a lot of strange stuff going on — Kim Dotcom was promising to reveal some dark secret about John Key, Nicky Hager's *Dirty Politics* came out of nowhere, Judith Collins was doing Judith Collins stuff, and David Cunliffe was being David Cunliffe. I really needed to be on top of my game.

Less than two weeks from the election I was walking on Upper Queen Street in Auckland, heading to the newsroom, when I felt a strange sensation in my right eye, like an electric shock. *What the fuck was that?* Then suddenly my vision went black and white in that eye. I wondered what it could be and then recalled that a few years earlier an ophthalmologist had mentioned something about the pressure in my eyes. Maybe it was something to do with that. I thought, *I've got to get this sorted quick, there's something fucking wrong here.*

I headed to the same ophthalmologist's offices, in Parnell. When I turned up, they said the guy had retired, but as I explained what was going on — that I could only see black and white out of my right eye — they ushered me in to see another specialist. She examined me and quite quickly said, 'You've got a detached retina.'

'A what?' The retina is at the back of the eye, the wall to the brain, responsible for decoding all the light that comes into the eye and turning it into an image. Sometimes it detaches from the eye itself, meaning the eye and the brain aren't linked properly. It was a really serious emergency because if the retina is detached for too long you can permanently lose your sight.

As I took in what she'd said, I jumped out of the chair, loosened my tie, opened the top button on my shirt and started striding around the room. I was sure she hadn't seen many people react this way. And I was sure she'd never had anyone say what I said next: 'No.'

She said the answer was most definitely 'yes', it had detached. Then came: 'You need an operation.'

And from me, again, 'no', and from her another definite 'yes'.

I still asked: 'Are you sure?'

'Yes,' she said.

'Am I going to be able to cover the election?' There was no 'yes' to this one from the ophthalmologist. So I tried again, from another angle: 'Are you sure it's detached?'

It was unbelievable that I was pushing back so much — here was a highly trained medical professional telling me I had this serious problem, one that could leave me permanently impaired, and I was interviewing her like a politician I thought was lying. 'Your sight is on the line,' she told me, calmly but directly. There was a short window to get it fixed. She got hold of the Greenlane Hospital eye clinic and they said they couldn't do it until the next night. 'Go home and rest and make sure you have that operation tomorrow night,' she told me.

I don't know how to explain this next bit, but I did not go home and rest. The next day, I went to work. Any normal person would have been at home, trying to relax and rest before this big operation. But we had a poll coming out, and I decided this was more important than my health. My only thought was: *I can get this poll done, go have the operation, and get back to the campaign trail and no one will notice I wasn't there.*

So I worked through the day with a detached retina, then presented live in the studio with one eye — by then, I was becoming known for my election countdown (which was Tova O'Brien's idea, by the way). 'There. Are. Ten. Days. To. Go.' I said those words, then jumped in a cab and went to Greenlane Hospital. I'd never been under anaesthetic before, so I was a bit worried about that. But my mind was obviously still thinking about politics because when I woke up I was jabbering away about Hone Harawira and the Internet Mana Party. Fortunately I hadn't just come up with it myself — apparently the surgical team had been talking about politics in the theatre so my subconscious mind must have tuned in.

During the operation, a vitrectomy, the retina was frozen back together with cryotherapy, and a gas bubble was pumped into my eye and pressed against the retina to hold it in place. The idea was that the bubble stayed there for a while, helping the retina repair itself, then the bubble gradually dissolved. It was a keyhole surgery through the front of the eye — an amazing operation. They'd only been able to do it for about 50 years — before it was available, people used to just go blind.

As expected, I woke up with no vision in the eye — it gradually returned — and spent the day in hospital. I asked the doctor about heading back to work and he said it was my choice — some people returned to light duties. So I checked myself out and returned to the campaign trail, fronting political show *The Nation* just three days after this delicate operation right next to my brain. It was an absolutely stupid thing to do.

I could barely see anything and felt pretty average. During the show, my fluorescent green hospital wrist band — which I hadn't even bothered to cut off — slipped from beneath my shirtsleeve; some sharp-eyed viewers wondered if I'd been at a rave or on a hydroslide.

”

The issue with my retina had nothing to do with stress — it was just bad timing. It turned out it was a genetic issue I was born with, and I was told there was a good chance it could happen in the left eye, too. I forgot about that pretty quickly.

But in February 2021, I had a sharp reminder. One day I noticed it was difficult to read the paper because there was a very tiny speckle of poor sight in my left eye. The ophthalmologist in Wellington had me in straight away given my history, and they were right. One quick look, and it was: 'Your retina is detaching.

You know the drill — the sooner we operate on it the better.' I was off to hospital that afternoon and had my other retina reattached, this time using laser surgery.

I'd dodged blindness a second time. Before discharging me, they said there was a small chance the retina could re-detach but, being me, I forgot about that pretty quickly, too. My eyesight started returning, and apart from a few problems along the way it seemed to be on the right track. But really, something just didn't feel right, like there was a huge drag on my body — unlike the first time when I recovered quite quickly.

Six weeks later I was in Auckland filming a scene that involved me staring at a laptop. I felt something was going wrong in the left eye again — the one that had just been operated on — but I didn't think of my retina because I'd passed the danger zone of it detaching again and had been given the all-clear. I was blinking my eye, testing the vision. The feeling I was experiencing was different to the other two times. I saw a couple of tiny black dots, and then a couple more. It was about four o'clock and I thought if I was going to see an ophthalmologist today I should move quickly — better to be safe than sorry and trying to find a hospital with a specialist at night-time.

More and more black things appeared in my eyesight. *Okay*, I thought, *this is getting urgent.* Since I was in Auckland, I figured I'd go back to the ophthalmologist I'd been to in 2014, in Parnell, the one whose office I'd marched around in, loosening my tie. So I looked her up, rang the reception and said it might be an emergency and that I was coming in. Even over the course of that phone call, things deteriorated. More and more black spots, getting bigger and bigger. *Fuck, this is bad.*

I called an Uber and got underway through the Auckland traffic. In the back of the car, things got worse and worse. Then, as we drove underneath the Khyber Pass motorway interchange, my left eye just went completely black. I couldn't see a thing out of it.

I felt terrible, too, so I said to the driver, 'If I faint, whatever you do, please wake me up when we get there — I need to get inside urgently.' Stuck in that traffic, I thought, *I don't know what's happened here, but I've gone blind in this eye. I've gone from having full sight an hour ago to having no sight at all. This is it. It's got me. I'll be permanently blind in one eye.* And then I fainted. I'm sure it was out of worry.

Next thing I knew, the driver was shaking me. 'We're here, brother, you've got to wake up.' Out of my one good eye, I looked around and realised we were not in Parnell where I was expecting to come. We were in another suburb, Remuera. I was shocked. *Oh my fucking God — we're in the wrong place.* But then I saw we were actually outside an ophthalmology clinic. When I'd entered the address in the Uber app, I'd obviously just put in the wrong place, in my panic. I figured that although I hadn't rung ahead at least I was at an eye specialist, so I went in.

I instantly got the fond and comforting feeling of being surrounded by old people. Anyone who has eye problems will know this feeling. The waiting rooms of ophthalmologists are filled with old people because most eye problems are age-related. I felt relieved to be in the right place. When I say relieved, it's all relative, right? I was still blind in one eye and had no idea what was going on. A specialist asked me what had happened. He grabbed his instrument and looked in my eye and immediately said, 'Okay, your retina has detached again.'

I fired questions, perhaps out of instinct, perhaps out of panic. Most importantly, I asked, 'Have I gone blind for good?'

He was calm and collected and said he'd contact Greenlane Hospital. 'There's still a chance we can save your sight.' He rang the hospital and asked if I could come straight in. The news was not good — I could not be operated on straight away because of the demand in the public system. I'd have to wait 24 hours, which is what had happened all those years ago. This time it was more urgent. This time I could not see anything. This time I was not in the mood to wait. Mentally, I was on a knife-edge. I did not want to go through life blind in one eye if I could avoid it.

The ophthalmologist said he could do the operation for me straight away, privately, and asked if I had health insurance. No, I did not. I asked how much it would cost. He told me a sum that would ordinarily have stressed me out, but I had no stress left to give. But I could not believe how much it was. The nurse, standing next to him, spoke up. *Phew*, I thought, *he's got it wrong.* He had got it wrong — the cost was actually higher.

It was quite the conundrum. In front of me was the prospect of waiting 24 hours in the public system and risking losing my sight forever — or shelling out a shitload of coin. I reverted to what I knew best: asking questions. 'What would you do if you were me?'

He gave a bit of a wishy-washy medical answer, sort of, 'I can't really advise you on what to do, blah, blah, blah . . .'

I turned on him like I had done many times before with prevaricating politicians, determined to get a straight answer. 'Come on, you've got to give me more.'

He paused for a second and said: 'If you can get this done, get it done — now.'

'Okay,' I said, 'let's get it done.'

Next came a moment of true Aucklandness. The anaesthetist had gone home for the day, and he was needed for the operation. 'He lives on the North Shore and I've got to get hold of him before he hits the Harbour Bridge.' Such an Auckland problem. Meanwhile I was standing in front of an Eftpos machine: you needed to pay upfront for operations not covered by health insurance. I did not have this particular sum of money in my everyday account, I was declined, and I was having trouble transferring it from another account, presumably because the TSB in Taranaki, where I'd banked since I was a kid, thought it looked suspicious.

The problem was it was now past five o'clock. The anaesthetist was on his way back from the brink of the bridge, the nurses who thought it was home time were all being held back, I was half blind, and I couldn't get hold of anyone at the bank. The stress in this scenario was just cranking up and up and up.

Eventually the ophthalmologist pulled rank and said he needed to do the operation and they would sort out the payment later. So we got underway. Previously, I'd been completely knocked out for the operation, but that wasn't possible this time because of the timing. So I'd have to have a local anaesthetic instead, which meant I'd be awake while they got inside my eye.

I had my third retina reattachment surgery, the second on my left eye in about six weeks. Afterwards, still in shock at what had unfolded over the course of a few hours, I sat in the recovery area with a cup of tea as everyone got ready to go home. Not long afterwards, the anaesthetist was on his way back to the North Shore and I had an eye patch on, ready to be discharged.

The only person I could think of who could come and get me in Auckland at that stage was Deol, the taxi driver who regularly took me to and from the airport when I was in town. So he came to sign me out. He stared at me, wondering what the hell was going on. 'I'll tell you in the car,' I said. 'It's a long story.'

Deol got me to my accommodation in Auckland for the night, but I needed to sort out a way to get home to Wellington. You can't fly for a while after these operations, with the gas bubble in the eye. Back in 2014, a guy who was at TV3 on work experience had to drive me down to Wellington.

Seven years later, I asked my Old Man to come and get me. He drove up from New Plymouth and we headed back to his place for the night. The plan was to rest up, but that night, about 24 hours after the operation, I actually went to the pub for a beer. I had virtually no vision — it takes about a month for it to come back properly. But I went to the pub. The next day we drove to Wellington and the first thing I did was go to the craft-beer place around the corner to stock up. It showed where my head was at. I'd had a massive escape, 'Paddy Luck' had kicked in yet again, and the first thing I thought of was getting on the booze.

”

I found out that the temporary blindness had been caused by a flooding of the eye when the retinal tear reopened. So while it had been very frightening, it was not as bad as it seemed. Just another drama for my eyes. They've been troublesome since I was a kid. I had to wear glasses or contact lenses from a young age because of short-sightedness, and I've got astigmatism that causes blurriness. As I got older, I needed reading glasses as well. All the surgery I've had done has caused me to get cataracts, so in 2024 I had to have both my lenses removed and replaced with artificial ones. That comes to a grand total of five major eye operations for me: three retina reattachments and two lens replacements. (In a bit of a Paddy Luck postscript, the new lenses have ended up giving me better sight.)

And there's more: in the lead-up to the 2017 election — so in between the two retina episodes — I was also diagnosed with glaucoma. It's unrelated to the other things, but it's another condition I've inherited through my genes. Pressure in the eye grinds away and causes damage to the optic nerve, which feeds information to your brain. It's called the silent thief of sight, as it takes your eyesight away bit by bit and you never get it back. Glaucoma does not have a cure, but the treatment I have been given — a small procedure in 2017 to relieve the immediate pressure, and daily medication since then — will hopefully prevent it from causing further damage.

Back in 2017, the specialists were not sure if we would get it under control, and it felt like a real blow at that time — just more things going wrong. I was making mistakes at work, I was getting angry at people, I was drinking way too much. Everything was compounding and compounding. *Okay, fuck — haven't I got enough on?* I thought. That feeling I had experienced years ago of my brain being squeezed and twisted, wrung tighter and tighter? As 2017 marched on, I was starting to feel like that again. And this time, it was really going to get me.

15.
THE WINSTON HANGOVER

The 2017 leaders debate was a massive high, and I really felt I'd pushed myself to another level. It gave me a surge of adrenaline afterwards. I hardly slept for days, my mind was just pulsating. But then the comedown hit — going back to my job as political editor on the campaign trail. Lisa Owen had made the genius call that I should step off the trail for a bit so I could properly prepare for the debate. The concentration required to get ready meant it would have been impossible to still be running around chasing stories, following leaders. But now I had to go back.

Before the debate, I'd been having those glitches in the machine — the missteps like the overly aggressive interview with James Shaw, and the volcanic blow-up at Andrew Campbell. On top of that, I wasn't handling the glaucoma diagnosis very well either. It was frightening, as people with glaucoma would know. But rather than deal with it, I reacted by putting it to the back of my mind and trying to ignore it. Not a great idea for someone who was in a shit headspace anyway.

After the debate, back on the daily grind of reporting on the campaign, I'd checked out. Instead of being microscopically across everything like a political editor should be, I was just, 'Oh, yeah, whatever.' It sounds really bad, I know. I thought I was hiding it. But after one particular day on the campaign, I went to the pub for a debrief with Jenna Lynch, who was in my gallery team along with the brilliant Lloyd Burr and excellent Isobel Ewing by then. Jenna is one of those insanely gifted political reporters who, like Tova, has X-ray vision, so I should have guessed she'd see through me. Over a beer I said how well they'd done without me there. She responded: 'You're just over this, aren't you?' She was right. I'd had a gutsful of the day-to-day admin of keeping on top of everything, making sure I had reporters and cameras in the right spots, making sure everything was covered. Let alone doing the actual journalism. Internally, I thought, *Yeah, you're right. I can't be fucked.* Looking back, it was the first time I'd thought about pulling the pin. Not that I was ready to admit it.

I'd seen politicians I'd covered go through the same decision-making process — coming to a realisation that time was up. The previous year, in October 2016, I'd been to the United Nations in New York with John Key. The political tectonic plates were shifting, and Key knew it. He'd won without Winston Peters in 2008, 2011 and 2014, and while National still had a lead in the polls over Labour, it was starting to look more and more likely that Peters would be back in the picture as a kingmaker come 2017. That probably gave Key nightmares, so the question about whether he'd stay on for another term became real. And his position publicly was, yes, he would. But my gut told me he wasn't solid.

In New York, I had the opportunity for an extended, sit-down interview with him and I thought, *I'm going to push him — will he stick around?* In these sorts of interviews, there was always a lot of pressure for your questions to not stray too far from the agenda of the trip — his advisers would be standing around in the room, and if you weren't asking about some boring-but-significant UN resolution or trade deal there'd be eye-rolling and a vibe that you were an uncouth imbecile. But I had a job to do, and so you could not be meek, no matter how awkward it felt.

The most uncomfortable example of this was when Key was in trouble for pulling the ponytail of a waitress at his favourite cafe. It was cringeworthy and he needed to respond to it — but the first real opportunity was during a pre-arranged interview at a palace in Turkey where we were on a state visit to mark the one-hundredth anniversary of Gallipoli. So during this time, which was all about the Anzacs and the relationship with Turkey, I had to sit down with him in this grand hall and say, 'So, about this hair-pulling . . .'

Anyway, there I was in New York after a trip to the UN, and I thought, *I'm going to go him about whether he's staying on.* His answers were a little bit different, and I sensed something had changed. So I had about four stabs at it. Of course I knew he wasn't going to just announce his resignation in this interview, but I thought I could maybe expose that he had delicately adjusted his position. Key was pretty good, though, and I couldn't hook him. Down on the street afterwards, I caught up with Corin Dann, from TVNZ, who'd also interviewed Key. I said to Corin that I should've pushed further because there was a subtle change in Key's language — not enough that I could definitely say he was going, but enough to think: *Hang on, something's up with Key.*

I got home exhausted after the trip and the year, and the bosses said I could have December 2016 off work. There wasn't much happening and the thinking was it would be good to recharge for the election year. I'd started relaxing at home, and on 5 December, a hot, sunny day, I was out the back mowing the lawn, earmuffs on. My phone was on the barbecue table and out of the corner of my eye, I saw it vibrating. I went over to check it and I'd missed five or six calls from Lloydy Burr. I rang him back.

'Key has called a mysterious press conference,' Lloydy said.

'When is it?'

'Twenty minutes.'

'Right, I'll see you.' I went inside, took my gumboots off, pulled my suit on, jumped into the car and went straight to the Beehive theatrette. I still had grass clippings in my hair.

I sat on the right-hand side — *Newshub* was always on the right, TVNZ on the left — and the room was abuzz. Nobody knew what was coming — there had been no clues other than it was a significant announcement. Of course we'd been speculating in the team — maybe there'd been an SAS casualty overseas, and they were fighting somewhere that we didn't know about? But honestly, we had no clue.

I heard the clicking of cameras in the corridor, so I knew Key must be approaching. I was immediately looking for clues. He came in carrying his notes like normal, but did seem a little nervous. No other minister was with him, which made me think, *Maybe it's about him?* Then as soon as he started talking, having been a student of his body language and words for eight years, I knew he was going. I texted the bosses back in the newsroom, 'He's resigning' just before he said it.

Key explained he'd told his wife, Bronagh, that he didn't really want the job anymore and he was struggling to answer questions about his future. Which was of course what was going on during that interview in New York. It was an example of how close I got to things as political editor, and how zoned in I was to everything, that I'd developed these instincts like a sixth sense. I never finished the lawns because it was straight into a leadership change, one of the biggest political yarns for a pol ed. Even though Key had anointed Bill English, there were machinations around who would take over as leader and deputy. It started getting messy and I was busy trying to expose the mess and show National was having the kind of shitstorm it hadn't had for ten years. It was time to figure out who was who in National's leadership zoo.

Then one of the MPs pulled me aside. 'I'm doing the numbers for Bill,' they reckoned. 'Doing the numbers' is one of those great political phrases — it meant counting up the votes for someone, a job usually reserved for some dastardly hard-arse. 'Bill has the numbers,' they went on. I was suspicious — you have to be, because sometimes it's just a tactic, putting the message out there, or inflating numbers, to persuade stragglers to come on board, or convince other contenders the race was over. So the numbers person took me into a side room and pulled out a list with a bunch of ticks and crosses. I'd been around a bit by this stage, this was not my first rodeo, and I knew this was the good stuff. English well and truly had the numbers. So it gave me the confidence to do my live cross that night saying English was going to be the next Prime Minister of New Zealand, a day ahead of the vote. *Bang*. I loved that feeling. In the zone, making big calls, getting them first, and getting them right.

”

But on the 2017 campaign, less than a year later, I was exactly the opposite. My instincts were off and my judgement was poor. One Friday, I'd agreed to judge a school talent quest and had a rare day out of the office. Jenna rang and said something strange had happened. An anonymous call had come into the *Newshub* gallery office, with the person saying there was an issue with Winston Peters' superannuation. There were enough details for it to sound entirely credible. I listened to her carefully, considered what she said, and asked a few questions. My reaction should have been to say, 'Okay, let's rip into this.' Instead, I was dismissive. 'Oh, yeah — how are we going to prove that?' My instinct was entirely wrong. I had completely lost the hunger, the political antennae. The Paddy of 2013, 2014, 2015 or 2016 would have been straight onto it. 'Let's get Peters and put it to him, let's put in the Official Information Act requests, let's go to ministers — everything.'

I was so out of tune, I didn't even give it a second thought. A little while later, I got invited to a late-night catch-up with someone who, as we call them in the trade, was a 'well-placed source'. This someone was actually 'an extremely well-placed source', the kind of meeting that as political editor you didn't turn down, because you might get some info. But as we sat there having a glass of wine, I couldn't figure out what it was about. I can now see there was a hint dropped to try to remind me about the leak. We were talking about how Peters might be back as kingmaker when the well-placed source said 'unless something comes out about him'. It was as if they knew the information had been passed on to me, a journalist seen as an attack dog. The trouble was the attack dog was asleep on the porch, and even that heavy hint didn't wake me.

It wasn't until late in the campaign when my old boss, Tim Murphy, now co-founder of the *Newsroom* website, tweeted one weekend that there was a '#motherofallscandals' coming on Monday that I was jolted into action. Finally I awakened. It had to be the Peters allegation. Lloydy rang Peters and put the claims to him; he didn't respond properly and we didn't quite have enough for the news that Sunday night. The yarn was on, though, there was still a chance for us to break it. But Peters knew the game was up, and front-footed things by releasing it himself after the 6 p.m. bulletin, issuing a statement confirming he'd been overpaid superannuation and had paid it back.

I had missed an absolutely massive yarn. It seemed to me there had clearly been an attempt to leak the story using the dark arts of politics — but although I'd known the information for weeks, I hadn't done anything with it. I'd fucked up. But I was a shell of myself around that time. I'd been doing weird stuff, like driving into work down the motorway and I didn't even have the energy to put my seatbelt on. Not because I had a death wish or anything, but because there was this lethargy. I was fried. But I was masking it. Once I got into work, the day would kick in and I'd be up again, pretending I was Paddy.

Booze was playing a big part, too. I was just so gung-ho, fuelled by alcohol. Once I accused Parliament's Speaker of putting lives at risk in a hyperbolic email sent after a day of heavy drinking. I'd been out at a seven-hour lunch on Ponsonby Road in Auckland with Toby Manhire, of *The Spinoff*, for an interview series they did sponsored by a wine company. We drank a lot, so much so that Toby 'crumpled in slow-motion to the floor' (as he wrote). Afterwards — while I was waiting for a butter-chicken curry in a food court — I was catching up with what had been going on back in Wellington.

There was a bunch of emails about an engineering report done about the state of the Press Gallery premises, following a series of earthquakes. The best response would have been to wait until the next day, acknowledge it, maybe ask some questions and seek some reassurance for my colleagues. Instead, perched in a food court, my brain soaked in booze, I concocted an email accusing the Speaker of endangering lives, and that it was time to 'tell the truth about what is going on'. And I hit send. I copied in a few bosses, too. To be fair, it didn't read like gibberish — I could function quite well on the piss. But it was a stupid email to send. I had completely overreacted. I woke up in the morning and thought, *Oh, boy. What have you done, PG?*

What I'd done was go nuclear. But by then I had a reputation for doing so, even without booze. Another time, there was a dispute over some pool coverage, where a TVNZ crew had filmed something that was supposed to be shared but never got to us on time. It was a big deal but there was a right way to handle it — and then there was the way I handled it. I went absolutely ape-shit. I just had no filter or ability to temper my response. I'd never been interested in Press Gallery internal politics — there's a committee drawn from its members that meets with the Speaker, for instance — but suddenly I was quoting arcane gallery rules to try to expel the person I believed was responsible. It was completely over the top and a bit insane. I was gathering evidence, constructing timelines, conducting interviews that were more like interrogations. I'd have heated meetings, acting belligerently, furiously demanding support for an expulsion motion. I forced poor Lloydy into it, seconding the motion. It was scandalous. Luckily, at the last minute, I pulled out.

I was plummeting. But that was who I'd become. The reaction to the footage dispute should have been, 'Hey, that sucks, but we'll sort this.' Instead it became an obsession. I was acting extremely weird.

”

Things were building and building, but the job rolled on. After the 2017 election, Winston Peters held both major parties to ransom for six weeks of coalition negotiations. I had some well-placed sources inside New Zealand First who were telling me there was no way Peters would go with National. They described it as 'utu' against National. Bizarrely, Peters would attack me for the stories in his typically florid way describing them as 'barefaced lies' — I say 'bizarrely' because I know how 'extremely well placed' my sources were. Not that I'm still bitter, but I'd like to point out that, while it wasn't known at the time, Peters had taken legal action against some National Party figures over the superannuation leak. Just saying. I'd also point out: let's just allow the outcome to speak for itself.

That outcome was announced in a theatrical speech during

the news hour on 19 October 2017 — when, in classic Peters style, he had the country on tenterhooks for seven minutes before saying he'd chosen Labour and making Jacinda Ardern prime minister. Talk about drama. It was chaotic afterwards with press conferences and reactions and special news bulletins. The next part of that routine was of course hitting the piss. We started drinking in the office and, with adrenaline, it didn't take long for the booze to hit.

It was getting late, but I jumped in a taxi to go and see the Greens, who were back in government, too, and were celebrating at a bar. Someone there gave me a tip that there was going to be a cannabis referendum. It was part of the deal, but no one knew about it yet so it was a scoop — I was even shown it in writing, so I knew all the details. *Bang*, I thought. *That's me in the morning.* I'd already been booked to appear on *The AM Show* and here I was with a scoop having raised many glasses — but barely a finger.

I was leaving the bar and looking for a cab, thinking, *Big day tomorrow. Huge day.* A guy was walking along the street, a punter, and he stopped me. 'Paddy, my bro, Winston is drinking down the road. I just saw him go up those stairs above The Exchange bar.'

'You serious?'

'Yeah, mate, private party.'

Well, I had to go and check it out, didn't I? I got to the stairs and there was a gate to stop people going into private functions, but there were no bouncers around so I opened the gate and went in. It was like a scene out of *The Sopranos* — Peters and his crew were in the corner of this big space, hunched around a table, smoking cigars and cigarettes. This was Peters out celebrating being back in government and who was going to stop him?

Over at the bar were Labour MPs Willie Jackson and Kelvin Davis. They slunk back into the shadows, like they didn't know if they were meant to be seen with Peters. The room went quiet and everyone looked at me. There was a stand-off, and one of Peters' crew came up a bit aggro and said, 'Get out of here, Gower — private function.'

Then Peters piped up. 'Let him in.' Peters waved me over. 'Come over here, come over here.' I was given a whiskey and a cigar, even though some of them still weren't happy I was there. Then Peters wanted to talk to me, so I sat by him, but he'd just look at me and smile and say, 'Paddy, Paddy, Paddy . . .' And that was it. Nothing. I thought he was going to get stuck into me about the 'utu' stories. But he just kept smiling and repeating 'Paddy, Paddy, Paddy . . .' and it would go no further. 'Paddy, Paddy, Paddy, Paddy, Paddy.'

That was the last thing I remembered of that night. I got so drunk, I completely blacked out.

I don't know how I got home, but I woke up, startled, to the sound of banging on the bedroom window. I still had my suit and tie on, and my shoes. I looked out the window and it was Matt Smith, my camera-operator mate.

'Bro, everyone's looking for you — you've got to get into work, they need you.'

'What do you mean?'

'It's two o'clock in the afternoon.'

I had missed all these calls on my phone. I had completely missed my *AM Show* slot — Duncan Garner even called me out on air saying, 'Paddy was last seen out drinking on Courtenay

Place. Call the police.' As fuck-ups go, this was a fuck-up for the ages.

I got to work and the vibe from the bosses was not good. There was no friendly 'Paddy, Paddy, Paddy'. Imagine it? In the middle of a huge political story, the political editor had gone missing, last seen out drinking on Courtenay Place. One of them said to me, 'We're going to need to talk about this, but get your story done first.' I made it to Ardern's press conference, and it led the 6 p.m. news bulletin.

But there was a bigger story going on for me, a personal one. I had a drinking problem and I was heading for a full-on breakdown.

16. BREAKING DOWN

Despite the fact I'd blacked out. Despite the fact I'd missed my slot on breakfast TV and been called out live on air. Despite the fact the bosses had to send a mate around to find me — despite all of that, I was still in denial about the Paddy I'd become.

I was arrogant. I felt untouchable. There was a little bit of shame, but not much. Mostly, I just thought: *What the fuck are they going to do? They can't do without me. They work me so fucking hard, they can't tell me what to do.* I was self-centred and had no perspective at all.

That made it tricky for the bosses; it seemed they didn't really know how to handle me. The only thing that happened from an employment sense was I had to apologise to *The AM Show* producer. No one mentioned apologising to Duncan Garner — probably because there was no way in hell I would have. I just got straight back into reporting on this new government.

But I was seriously disengaged.

The weekend after the government formed, one of Jacinda Ardern's staff called. 'The boss wants to talk to you. She's going to ring soon, okay?' I hadn't really talked with Ardern much in her career. During all the machinations within Labour — the switching of leaders, and the coups — I had a lot of sources leaking me info. Ardern never got involved in that dirty stuff. She rigidly never spoke to me about it, not even off the record, and never seemed that interested in courting political journos. The closest she came to talking to me about any of that stuff was one night after a Labour Party conference when she was a junior MP. I was in a bar and she was on the other side with some of her supporters, which was basically every young or youngish Labour activist ever born. One of them came over to say Ardern believed I thought she didn't have what it took to be leader one day and sounded me out as to why. I didn't think that, by the way, but it was very strange — like a word being sent via an emissary of some emperor.

Anyway, back at home after the 2017 election, the phone rang and it was Prime Minister Ardern on the line. I went into the garden to speak with her. This was the new PM ringing me and I should've been fully in the zone. As political editor it was important to establish a relationship with the PM. Key used to ring regularly, sometimes just for background, sometimes pure spin. I always took the call and I was always focused — it was a critical pipeline. But on the phone with Ardern, I wasn't interested in a single word she had to say. I was polite, but I just didn't care. I was thinking, *These people all sound the fucking same.*

She was heading to APEC in Vietnam, where she was going

to meet US President Donald Trump, and I was going over, too. I should have been thrilled. Far from it. Another air-force flight, another dose of alcohol at altitude. In my seat, I started feeling paranoid and had this burgeoning sense of doom. I was even struggling to breathe properly at times. There was no particular reason; it was just extreme apprehension and anxiety.

Once we were on the ground, I felt a bit better and slipped into the routine. Another PM's overseas trip. Another APEC. Rinse, repeat. I was on remote control. Every time I was on my own, though, the paranoia and doom crept back.

One night, I was lying on my bed in a hotel in Da Nang, a city in central Vietnam. I'd taken sleeping pills but they weren't working. The hotel was a place where American servicemen used to go for R&R during the war. It had shutters and a big ceiling fan swooping in circles, making futile attempts to shoo away the hot air. I watched it go around and around and I could see the pattern of my life. Around and around, chasing politicians, getting nowhere, sucking the life out of me.

Now this might seem a bit random but I recalled a scene in my favourite movie, *Heat*, which came out in 1996. It featured Al Pacino and Robert De Niro — the first time they appeared on screen together. Pacino played a cocaine-fuelled cop pursuing a master criminal, played by De Niro, both characters brilliant at what they did, and both of their lives unravelling. Eventually the two of them came face to face in a cafe and they confided in each other, and Pacino's character told his arch rival that his life was disintegrating, 'because I spend all my time chasing guys like you around the block'.

I stared at the fan and had a sense of dread about the

Parliamentary term ahead, doing the same things over again, chasing the same guys around the same block. I thought there was no way I could drag myself through to the 2020 election. And then I thought there was no way I could do another year of this job. Then I thought there was no way I could come back to the job in the New Year. Then I thought there was no way I could make Christmas. And then I thought, actually, there was no way I could come back tomorrow.

I could not face the thought of putting my suit on in the morning, of picking up a microphone, of getting in front of a camera. I searched for an Air New Zealand flight home, and was ready to pay a taxi driver for the 900-kilometre trip to Ho Chi Minh City to get it. I wasn't going to tell anyone, I was just going to go, and say I had come down crook. There were no tears, no tantrums, just a realisation that I couldn't do this job anymore. I was over it.

Matt Smith, the cam op with whom I had shared so many adventures, was on the trip, too. I had a yarn with him, he knew something was up, but not quite what. I managed to pull myself back from the brink of escaping the country. I decided I would finish off the trip — after APEC, Ardern was going to the Philippines on the way home — and then that would be it.

I had an interview to do with Ardern in Manila, which I knew would be my last one as political editor. It was a weird frame of mind but I wanted to go out strong.

Then, straight after, Ardern was meeting with Rodrigo Duterte, the Philippines' president, on the other side of town. According to the schedule, and the traffic, it was going to be impossible to get there without the special escort that Ardern had. Then, from inside my broken mind there was a surge of energy. I turned to Matt and said, 'Let's go.' We went on this crazy cross-town race involving a bus, golf cart, and quite a lot of running, even dashing through a hotel kitchen, waved on by Filipino officials directing us to the room where the photo op was due to take place. We burst through a side door, and there was Duterte and a room full of Filipino journalists and cameras, and, right then, in walked Ardern. We'd made it. Duterte started rambling about a trip to Auckland where he'd gone to a fish shop. I cracked up. It was crazy and perfect. What a way to go out.

I did one last live cross, then headed straight up to the rooftop bar. I drank gin and tonic after gin and tonic and got absolutely shit-faced. My career was over. And as far as I was concerned, it wasn't just the political editor job, or *Newshub*. It was journalism. There would be no more fucking news.

"

I still hadn't told the bosses. On the flight home we stopped off in Darwin and I rang a few people close to me, hinting at what I was thinking and looking for reassuring advice. They all said I should just have a break, and definitely shouldn't quit. I quickly decided their advice was crap. My mind was made up.

When I got home, I rang Hal Crawford, the head of news, and said I wanted a meeting away from the TV3 office somewhere so nobody would see us. We met in a cafe, along with Richard Sutherland, Hal's deputy. I told them: 'I'm resigning immediately, I've had a gutsful.' And they looked scared. Not about the work — about me. They could tell they were looking at an unwell person, and they were very caring towards me. Hal wanted to know why. It was a good question. And it just came out: 'The burden. It's just the fucking burden.' That was the answer, it was the burden I was carrying. I thought it was the job — I didn't realise it was so much more. Undoubtedly they would have had their corporate hats on, thinking this would not look good, but I could tell they were worried about me, too. I'd dropped a bombshell on them, that I was quitting journalism.

Richard said, 'Just don't do it today — don't send an email. Promise us you'll do it tomorrow.' The next morning they were in touch: 'You can leave the pol ed job. But just stay working here.'

'What will I do?'

'We don't know yet — we haven't had much time. But we'll figure something out.'

Within 24 hours, they came up with the idea of a roving-reporter role. They said I could report on stories around the country, but that I wouldn't have to come back to Parliament. It gave me hope. The idea of talking to real Kiwis, of going around the country — everywhere but that one square kilometre around Parliament, the place that had destroyed me — appealed. They told me I could take three months off, then return as 'national correspondent'.

I've got to say that Hal and Richard dealt with the situation bloody well, the work stuff and the personal concern. They saved my career, and gave me a second chance. And by doing that, they saved me.

”

I could not face being in the Press Gallery one more day, so they agreed to announce that I was stepping down as soon as possible. But there are always complications. The day it was due to happen, I got a call from Richard telling me TV3 had an announcement planned around *Dancing with the Stars* and corporate comms did not want my news to come out on the same day because that would overshadow *DWTS*. So I very reluctantly delayed it by another 24 hours. Which meant I had to keep hiding it from my team: Jenna, Isobel and Lloyd.

I ran the usual morning meeting with them in the gallery office the next day, in my suit. Then I told the three of them, 'I've just got to go and see a man about a dog.' Those were my exact words, that was the best I could come up with. I couldn't even invent a decent bullshit excuse. Everyone in Wellington was called to a meeting at the TV3 building in Walter Street, the main Wellington newsroom. I was hiding in an edit suite as everyone arrived, and I'd changed out of my suit into brand-new casual clothes, jeans and a shirt I'd picked up on my way across town. It felt symbolic, and to be honest I was pretty certain there would be drinks later.

The gallery team, being newshounds, figured something was up and started asking the bosses: 'Is Paddy resigning?' When everyone was ready I stepped out of the edit suite. Unusually for me, I'd written out a speech. I'd clearly seen too many Winston Peters announcements over the years because, to be honest, it was a bit overly dramatic, drawing on how I hoped I'd lived out the hopes and dreams of my grandmother. I talked about the Kiwi dream. Flourishes like that. It was a big occasion, sure, but when it came down to it I was just changing jobs and here I was carrying on with soaring oratory like I was Obama. I saw people either crying or confused. I didn't let on the real reason I was leaving, instead saying it was just time, after a decade in the gallery.

At the pub afterwards, to my surprise, a TV was wheeled in. In the few hours since the announcement, Jenna had worked her butt off making a leaving tape — it's a tradition for people when they finish up at TV, a montage of big moments on screen and bloopers. Even though I wasn't leaving *Newshub*, they'd gone to the trouble of doing this. It showed me they really cared for me, and was truly humbling — the ultimate TV salute.

"

The truth was I was having a breakdown. I was paranoid that people would find out. I'd gone back to the psychologist, but other than that I hunkered down for the summer. I spent a lot of time in the sun and drank a lot of craft beer. Dad came and stayed and we hung out in the garden, pulling out weeds, cutting back plants, and one of the few things I went out for was to take rubbish to the dump. I figured that by leaving the job I'd avoided people finding out what was really going on, and that after a break I'd go back to work and it would all be sweet.

I eventually had to come back to my new role as national correspondent. I didn't have a yarn, but Christchurch producer Kate McCallum sure did: she'd amassed a box of documents that contained an amazing story about how Christchurch earthquake insurance claimants were being spied on by private investigators working for a government-owned insurer. It was an important story — ordinary Kiwis being spied on. It was important to me, too; it meant I was back, kind of anyway, even though I hadn't properly dealt with the underlying problems. And then I had to face harsh realities. I hadn't realised that, as political editor, there were a lot of people doing things for me. I'd been waited on hand and foot in the workplace for five years. Now I was operating on my own a lot. Most of the time there was no one to bounce ideas off, no camaraderie. It felt like a lonely grind.

Furthermore, I was struggling with no longer being the centre of attention. As political editor, I was right in the middle of things and everyone looked to me. The reality was I'd developed a massive ego. I thought that stepping away from the job would solve everything. But of course it hadn't, especially the ego problem. I was miserable, back to feeling like I had when I returned from overseas, like I had when Mum was dying. I was lost.

"

During that time, though, I discovered things about myself. I'd hooked into a gig as a guest presenter on *The Project*, and one week they were concentrating on the topic of addiction. We were in a meeting and the anchor, my friend Jesse Mulligan, asked in an almost throwaway fashion if I wanted to say something about why I'd left the gallery. I said to him I'd been a workaholic — that was how I first characterised what I'd been through. Jesse and the show's boss, Jon Bridges, looked at me with wide eyes. It was the first time I'd ever let on there was something more to me leaving the job. They asked if I'd say that live on the show, and I said I'd see.

When I told the studio audience I'd struggled with an addiction — to journalism and politics — they laughed. But Jesse steered things back to the seriousness of my words, and I said how work had infected all areas of my life. I said I was 'starting to hate' the job. It was not the whole truth, but it was out there. I was really surprised by the public reaction, with lots of people saying they'd had no idea, and they'd had similar problems. It was before things like 'burnout' were spoken about much, and I'd really connected with people.

It made me think I wasn't alone. It was a weird way to do it, on national TV, but it became the start of something much bigger for me around opening up. It led me into a different place, a new Paddy, of being vulnerable, of owning stuff and talking about things that people didn't talk about. And it had only happened because Jesse asked me if I had anything to say.

Soon afterwards, I was at the journalism school at Canterbury University, talking to students about telling powerful TV stories. I discussed at length one particular example, getting deep and technical about how we'd pulled the story together. At the end, I opened up for questions and there were a few of the standard ones, and then a student said: 'I'd like to get into TV like you, but I don't want to because I'm worried about what people would say about the way I look.' I could see other students nodding and it went really quiet. This was the question they really wanted an answer to.

So I told her that over the years people had said so many awful things about the way I looked. 'Imagine everything I would've missed out on, all the stories I wouldn't have told, all the adventures I wouldn't have had, if I'd stopped because of

ABOVE Inside the Pike River mine with Bernie Monk, 2018. We are in the mine's entry tunnel, facing the concrete plug that would be ripped down when re-entry happened. Bernie told me afterwards that he felt like tearing the wall down himself. Camera op Bob Grieve took a series of amazing photos like this on an old-school film camera, as we weren't allowed any electronics inside. *Bob Grieve*

RIGHT PG the full-blown alcoholic in 2019. I look like shit in this photo, and that's because booze was making me look and feel like shit.

ABOVE With some of my friends at Al Noor mosque. We're sharing the Iftar meal at sunset during Ramadan, just two months after the March 2019 shootings.

RIGHT Filming *Patrick Gower: On Weed* in 2019 meant that I got to see a lot of weed plants. These specimens belong to Gandalf, a bearded hippie who hadn't worn underpants in 40 years. He taught me a lot about the plant's incredible powers. *Ruckus*

TOP Meeting Sir Bob Elliott, the medical genius who got me campaigning for cystic fibrosis sufferers in New Zealand to have access to the miracle drug Trikafta. I never saw Sir Bob again; he died in August 2020, not long after this shot was taken. It was awesome to help with one of his final wishes.

ABOVE On set for *Patrick Gower: On Booze* in late 2020, with my friend and former competing political editor Corin Dann. Our scene together got intense when Corin called out my problem with booze. In the moment I rejected this, but that would soon change (see page 235). *Ruckus*

RIGHT In hospital after my left retina detached in early 2021. I've had three retina reattachment operations, which is quite a lot given we humans only have two retinas (one of the ops had to be repeated). A detached retina can cause permanent blindness, so I count myself lucky to still be able to see.

BELOW Holding 1 kilogram of methamphetamine (street value about $500,000). This haul was uncovered during a customs inspection while filming *Patrick Gower: On P* in 2021. Meth has been around for my entire career, but we need to do something about it more than ever before. *Ruckus*

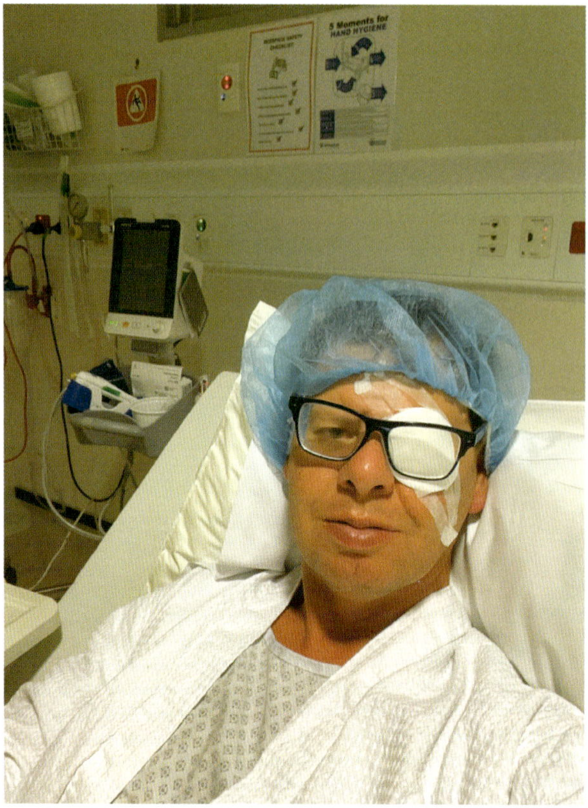

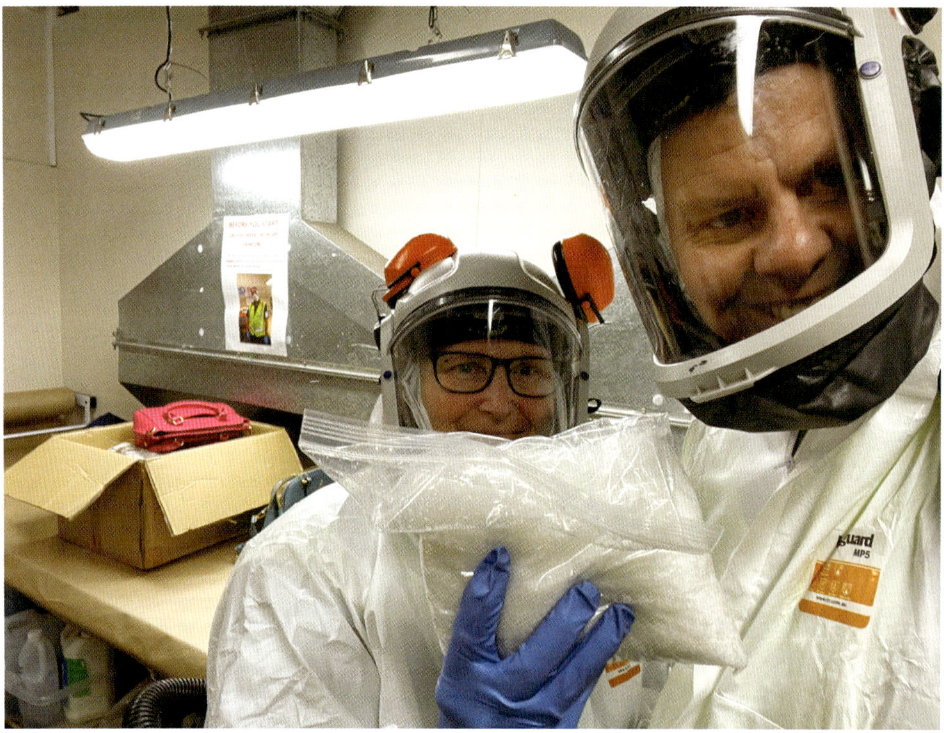

TOP Beaming in from Westminster Abbey before the Queen's funeral in September 2022. It is hard to believe but in this sombre environment I dropped another f-bomb on live TV! *John Fleming*

ABOVE On the shiny new set of *Paddy Gower Has Issues* in early 2023, with comedian Karen O'Leary. It was a dream come true having my own show. *Warner Bros. Discovery*

LEFT About to get very cold. I'm in the back of a US Air Force plane on the way to Antarctica in 2023. *Ruckus*

BELOW Standing on top of Observation Hill in Antarctica beside the cross erected in memory of explorer Robert Falcon Scott and his men, who died on their way home from the South Pole. The inscription on the cross comes from Tennyson's poem 'Ulysses', and I took huge inspiration from its words (see page 249).

ABOVE Moderating the leaders debate in the lead-up to the 2023 New Zealand general election. This was my third debate, following campaigns in 2017 and 2020. I love being out in the middle on behalf of Kiwis. Greg Bowker / *Warner Bros. Discovery*

RIGHT Big celebrations after winning Best Presenter: News and Current Affairs at the 2023 New Zealand Television Awards. Things were going so well, it seemed too good to be true — and it was. Within a couple of months, my show was put on hold and we were informed of the proposal to shut down *Newshub*. *NZTVA*

TOP I was proud to think I got smashed in this tackle from former All Black prop John Afoa during a charity rugby match in January 2024, held in honour of the late cancer-care campaigner Blair Vining. Then I saw this photo and realised Afoa was just having a laugh! *Debbie Fahey*

ABOVE This Rod Emmerson cartoon ran in the *New Zealand Herald* on 11 April 2024, the day after the *Newshub* closure was confirmed. It is pretty hard case to go from having my name in the paper as a lowly night-duty reporter to being cartoon fodder alongside my famous quote! *Rod Emmerson*

what people said about how I looked.' I told them that from the moment I'd walked in the room, I'd never once thought about how any of them looked, and they shouldn't let worrying about their looks stop them from using their talents and chasing their dreams.

It was the first time I'd ever spoken about this stuff, about how self-conscious I was, about how I hated people talking about how I looked.

I think it was meant to be, because the next time I was on *The Project*, they were doing a bullying segment, and once again I was asked if there was anything I wanted to say. I said, yeah, there was. And I opened up about how it started with 'Paddy Carrots', and how people had teased me, ran me down, mocked me about my looks. It blew up, and was one of the biggest things I'd ever done on TV. It showed me how I could articulate what many people were going through but couldn't say themselves. That I shouldn't be afraid to say things, because I could be saying them for other people. And it was the start of a new nickname: the Oversharer-in-Chief.

It also marked a turning point for me. I was 40 and had finally acknowledged that I'd still been worrying about the way I looked. When I spoke about it publicly, it broke the hold it had over me. I wasn't going to care what people thought anymore. It was the beginning of a new me. I'd discovered that confronting these things in public was giving me the power to fight my own demons.

17.
INTO PIKE RIVER

The Pike River disaster was on 19 November 2010 — that's the day the mine exploded and 29 men got trapped inside. But pinning it to one date feels wrong to me, because it has just been this long, slow, grinding tragedy that has never stopped causing grief for the families of the victims, the people of the West Coast, and the country.

I was at work in the Press Gallery as a relatively new *3News* political reporter on the day. Mark Jennings rang asking if I could get down to the West Coast. I was surprised because I was a politics specialist and not used to reporting in the field for TV, but obviously I was keen to get on such a big breaking story.

I flew down with Michael Morrah, and our first job was to cover a briefing for the family members soon after the disaster. They'd been called to a meeting in a Greymouth hall, a bunch of Coasters trying to get their heads around what had happened to their sons, husbands, fathers and uncles. Morrah and I set about trying to find family members. I saw this guy walking across the car park, a head of white hair and the vibe of a down-to-earth leader, like a rugby captain or coach; someone people would listen to. I introduced myself and he said he'd talk to me after the meeting, which he did — and he's been talking to Kiwis ever since. That was Bernie Monk.

Bernie and his wife, Kath, lost their son Michael in the mine. Over the following years, I formed a real bond with Bernie. The more time I spent with him, the more I liked him. We had a bit in common — he'd gone to a Catholic school, too, St Pat's Silverstream — and I'd met his two other kids and got on bloody well with them. He owned a pub, and one day we were sitting in his bar and I said something about how hard it must be to be surrounded by alcohol all day, that you'd always want to get on the booze. He said: 'I don't drink — I haven't had a drink since Pike River. I just knew that if I wanted to fight for Michael I'd need all my brain and all my energy.' I sipped on my beer and said, 'Interesting.' I was still a heavy drinker at the time, and to be honest I wasn't really interested and didn't take the conversation further.

Bernie and I kept in regular contact, and every time there was a development I'd get down myself or make sure we got a camera to him. When I held my ear against the door before the leaders debate in 2017 and heard Bill English say I was obsessed with Pike River, he was damn right. I'd followed this story closely, and at that election one of the live issues was about re-entry to the mine — it was something Winston Peters campaigned on.

Re-entry was a big deal, because nobody had ever tried. It was always claimed to be too dangerous, too hard, too expensive, too late — any and every excuse had been used since the day of the explosion. It didn't matter that there could have been survivors in there, or that bodies could have been recovered, or crucial evidence secured. The government had even tried to seal it permanently. In 2018, in my new role as national correspondent, I closely followed the twists and turns of whether a re-entry would be possible. Finally, with Peters in government, and Andrew Little appointed the minister responsible for overseeing the re-entry, there was progress. They were going to open up the 2.4-kilometre drift — like a passageway into the mine — and have a look.

Bernie and I spoke about going into the drift. You could walk 30 metres into the drift before you hit a concrete plug (put in after the blast), so it was like a big cave. It would be a symbolic visit, the first time Bernie had gone, and the first time a journalist had been into the mine. After some back and forth, it was all signed off by the re-entry team that we could walk up to the cap, an 88-centimetre-thick plug of concrete. Bernie's boy, Michael, and the other men were on the other side — this would be the closest he would've been to his son in eight years.

As we prepared, the re-entry team's boss Dinghy Pattinson flew me up to the mine in a helicopter to explain how they were going to undertake the dangerous task of getting into the mine itself. I'd been coming to the Coast for years and it had really found a place in my heart. It reminded me of Taranaki — the rugged coastline and the people who were determined and independent. As we flew over Greymouth, 'The Barber' was out — a chilly, damp wind you see as well as feel; as it blasts down the Grey Valley it forms a misty low-lying cloud. It gets its name because the cloud looks like a beard, but also because it's so cold it could cut you in two. To see it from the sky was awesome: it looked like it was standing guard over the town as we were about to visit those fallen sons of the Coast.

”

Approaching the shaft with Bernie was always going to be emotional, but it wasn't until we started to get close that the magnitude hit me. We saw the clipboard where the miners had left their ID tags — the tags of those who didn't make it out remained hanging where they'd left them on the day of their last shift. It was a scene shown on TV hundreds of times. But to be standing there with Bernie, whose son had put one of those tags up on the board during his final moments above ground, was full on.

In all the years I'd known him, I'd never seen Bernie cry. But in the corner of his eye, I saw a tear. It really hit me. Until then, I'd been thinking about the physical danger — things like the methane levels at the site. But the reality was there was nothing hazardous about what we were doing, given all the precautions we were taking. I switched to worrying about Bernie — what had I got this guy into? We asked Bernie if he still wanted to do this. Dinghy, a hell of a good bloke from a family of coalminers, said, 'Bernie, you all good, mate?'

He just said 'yep', and the next thing we were going in — Bernie, Dinghy, camera operator Bob Grieve and me.

We got to the cap and Dinghy said, 'Bernie, you can have a minute alone.' And we just stood back. It was getting heavy, heavier than the Paparoa Range above us. We were inside the mine, in the dark, and in front of us was the lonely frame of Bernie Monk. In many ways, he'd become the face of the families, a public figure. But as he stood there, he was a grieving dad. There was a piece of reinforcing steel jutting out of the concrete and he lifted his hand to it and gripped it, like he was trying to grab hold of all that lay on the other side.

One of the rules was that we weren't allowed to take lights or our regular TV camera into the mine — anything with batteries — due to the danger of explosion. We'd come up with the idea of using an old film camera, and Bob had tracked one down and figured out the logistics of how he could pull it off in this dark place. As Bernie stood there, Bob wound the film on and took the photo. It was so silent, the clicking noise of the camera reverberated. We had no idea if it had worked, either — and we wouldn't until the film was developed.

Back outside the mine, I interviewed Bernie, asking him what he had been thinking as he stood there. 'I wanted to tear the wall down myself.' It was incredibly moving. He said it like he really meant it, and I reckon he would have tried if we had left him there. Bernie had fought and fought to get back into that mine. Everything had been stacked against the 29 men since before the first day — there were so many problems with the mine from day one. Then came all the crap Bernie and the families had to face afterwards, up against insurmountable odds, up against the machine of the corporate world and the government, layers and layers of bureaucracy who wanted them to stop. But Bernie never stopped, never gave in. When things get hard for me, sometimes I think of him. Bernie keeps fighting for his son, no matter how hard it gets. That's what I'd want my Old Man to do for me. And that's why Bernie Monk is one of my heroes. He'd fought for his son and the others against all odds.

You can call what happened at Pike River — and what continues to happen — all sorts of things: a national shame, a stain on our country's history. But I call it something else: a cover-up. Not by anyone in particular, or any particular organisation, but a cover-up nonetheless. There have been so many poor decisions and they've been buried; so many barriers preventing the families from getting what they want. They should have been allowed to get those bodies from the get-go.

I've interviewed hundreds of families who've lost loved ones in all sorts of tragic circumstances. There is one thing they all want: some kind of closure. We've left these Pike River families without that. It's a fucking disgrace.

Bernie deserves to have his son back. All those families do.

Bob and I found a camera shop in Christchurch, dropped off the film from the old-school camera and explained it was very important. We had to wait for an hour, so we nipped to the pub next door for a beer, knowing a lot rested on what we'd find when we went back. We walked into the shop and the guy was smiling. We opened up the envelope and there it was: a photo of Bernie Monk up against the concrete wall of the Pike River mine with his hand around a piece of reinforcing steel. It was the most amazing picture I'd ever seen.

"

There's another reason the Coast and Pike River have become so much a part of my story: I very nearly came a cropper out in the bush there during a crazy trip with some mates. Ever since our schooldays at Francis Douglas, a group of us have stayed tight, like brothers. We like to do stuff together, and one weekend in 2022 we headed to the West Coast to do some bike riding. I'd only just taken up cycling, and we competed in a race around Lake Brunner, my first competitive road race. During the race, we bunched up in a peloton in our custom-made lycra in school-uniform colours. It was exhilarating to be flying through the West Coast bush with mates, just like how we used to take on the headwind on our way to school back in the day.

There was, however, a horror throwback to my life as a political reporter: the Speaker of the House, Trevor Mallard, was riding, too. Making it worse, he beat me. I was in my honeymoon phase with cycling and thought it was cool — but then I saw Mallard and he kind of wrecked that.

We had a day's rest and I took the boys to meet Bernie at the Paroa Hotel. We were going to do a mountain-bike ride across a section of the Paparoa Range you could ride in a day, alongside the Pike River. Given the special significance it had for me, I wanted to share that with them, too. But the ride was cursed from the very beginning. We'd arrived on the Coast to news the track was closed because of a slip. However, a photo of the slip started circulating in a middle-aged cyclists' underworld showing it wasn't too bad and there were rumours people had been able to get through. That was kind of cancelled out by talk that there were some workers setting up explosives to clear the slip. And now the weather was packing in again, making the ride starting to look extremely dicey.

We had a meeting in a local pub known as 'Formerly The

Blackball Hilton', and reviewed the evidence: the fact the track was closed; the fact there was a slip; the fact there could be explosives; the fact the weather was deteriorating; the fact it was May and the daylight hours were limited; the fact some of us were inexperienced; the fact we'd already just had an arduous ride. The decision was obvious. We pushed go.

And so, the next morning, we set off into the Paparoa Range. I found it hard from the first pedal. There was a lot of uphill riding and parts of the track had washed out. We made it to the first hut, which would have been a good place to turn back. We had a mature discussion about options, which quickly became an argument with some abuse hurled, and some of the group just rode off. The rest of us couldn't afford to be left behind so we all eventually set off, too. We didn't have time to dither — the ride we'd embarked on, from Blackball to Punakaiki, was always going to be tough. And with the extra pressure of getting it done before dark, every second counted.

After a while, we regrouped near the top of the ranges, and I went to take a photo — I love taking photos on my phone — but that did not go down well as it was considered time-wasting by some, and more abuse was hurled. Everyone was feeling the pressure, and there were still plenty of punishing climbs and tricky downhills. I decided to deal with it like I used to with that headwind when I was a kid, swearing at the world, whereas others handled it differently. My mate Nathan went completely silent. He was in the zone. Others shouted encouragement and absolute lies, things like the hills were nearly over. And of course there was more abuse.

At another hut we debated whether we should stay the night,

especially since we had absolutely no idea if we could get across the slip and would have to turn back for the hut if we didn't. I was having visions of a rescue, or being caught on this closed track, and news crews, including my colleagues, waiting at the bottom, just like that trip to the mountain when we were kids and it flooded. Except I knew this time the headlines would be about this idiot Gower having to be rescued and wasting everybody's time after riding a closed track in a storm.

We cracked on. I didn't even suggest to the guys we stop for a photo at a picturesque waterfall we came across. I'd learnt my lesson. On the downhills, my forearms were so fatigued from hanging on that they turned to jelly. The only thing that kept me going was my mate Hammy, who'd been assigned to get me home. He decided to do this with next-level tough love — riding behind me with yet more abuse, effectively whipping me along like he was driving a chariot. 'Just fucking ride, PG! Just fucking ride!'

All the time, we were heading towards a slip, towards the unknown. As we reached it, we saw we could get across and it wasn't rigged with the explosives we'd been warned about. We let out loud whoops as we helped each other get our bikes across. Unfortunately, our noise attracted the work gang camped nearby and we heard the sound of their quad bikes heading our way to find out what the hell was going on. The fear of getting busted took hold, and it gave me the biggest burst of energy to get out of there. Near the end, darkness set in and we needed torches to see. We only had two between the six of us. So the last few kilometres we had to push our bikes on foot, before finally emerging at the Punakaiki hotel.

Stupid? Yes, absolutely. Fun? No, definitely not. A good yarn? Hell yeah.

”

It also created an extra-special memory. In the group on that trip, about half of us were in on a secret. Our mate Nathan had been diagnosed with cancer, but he was keeping the news extremely private. Some months earlier, I'd twigged something was up, and he'd reluctantly told me, but he didn't want any sympathy — he just wanted to get on with his life. So he asked me not to tell anyone. Of course I honoured that, not even telling some of our mutual close friends on the ride.

When he gave me the news, I asked him what kind of cancer he had, what his prognosis was — the usual questions. He didn't want to say much, but he told me he had bowel cancer.

Nathan was a hero of mine for lots of reasons, and his unusual approach to cancer was one of them. He hid it from everyone for as long as he could, and tried to fight it for as long as he could. He took the pain of the cancer and then the treatment to fight it and never let it show, to protect the people he cared about. He died eighteen months after telling me. I gave the eulogy at his funeral and compared the way he fought cancer to how Francis Douglas refused to give in to torture — they both took the pain to protect people they cared about.

I had to head to Auckland the morning after the funeral to prepare for the 2023 leaders debate, my third time moderating. Once again I had a top team: Todd Symons was joined by outstanding researcher Natasha Bull and young gun reporter

Zane Small. But it was only two weeks away, one of my best mates had just died, and I was really struggling to get up for the debate. So I thought of doing something in honour of Nathan. I was going to fight for bowel-cancer patients like him. Screening for bowel cancer in New Zealand was far behind what it was in Australia, and I was determined to seek a commitment from the leaders, Labour's Chris Hipkins and National's Christopher Luxon, to lower the screening age from 60 to 45, so people didn't have to die like my friend had.

I took Nathan's funeral pamphlet into the debate and put it on the lectern, so when I looked down I saw a smiling picture of my mate. I knew the bro would take me straight into the ninety-ninth percentile, and did he what! I was in the zone all night. From time to time, I'd put my hand down on him, as if I was holding him by the shoulder. Even if no one else knew, he was there with me. I was going to make sure this was going to be part of Nathan's legacy.

I ripped into it, and sure enough both of the leaders promised to lower the screening age. I took a deep breath, nodded to a woman in the audience who had bowel cancer herself and also looked down at Nathan. It was a powerful, private moment for me in such a public arena.

I heard from Bowel Cancer New Zealand, who were ecstatic about the leaders debate and asked if I would help front a campaign. Missy Vining, wife of the late bowel-cancer campaigner Blair Vining, got hold of me, too, impressed with my passion for the cause. She asked if I'd captain a team in the annual charity-fundraiser rugby match in honour of Blair. I didn't want a bar of it, but I knew Nathan would have a laugh about the former

Francis Douglas Fourth XV captain leading a team of former All Blacks and Super Rugby stars, so of course I agreed.

I rang Nathan's widow to check she was okay with me campaigning for bowel cancer. 'Hold up, PG. There's something I have to tell you.' It turned out Nathan didn't even have bowel cancer — he had pancreatic cancer. He'd only told me and others he had bowel cancer because he knew I'd search pancreatic cancer online and see that it had a low survival rate. He was trying to protect us.

I was a little shocked at first. Yet when I hung up, I started laughing my head off. At least I had secured a cross-party commitment — one that I will make sure they stick to. But it was too late to get out of my own commitment — to Missy Vining and the rugby game. I was shitting myself, thinking I'd get smashed. My tactic was to avoid getting tackled at all costs. At one point, former All Black Jason Eaton made a break and threw a miracle off-load to me out in the open. With 10,000 Southlanders watching, I had no choice but to catch it. As soon as I did, I looked up and saw former All Black front-rower John Afoa lining me up. I braced for impact, took the tackle, and managed to stand up afterwards, unbroken.

I was quite proud of myself — until I saw a photo the next day showing Afoa was laughing and had tackled me like a teddy bear. Nathan would have pissed himself. I can imagine him cracking up about the whole thing I'd got myself into, campaigning for bowel cancer when he didn't even have it. It was like he'd unintentionally played his final prank on me and I could never get him back for it. You got me good, my brother.

18.
HAUNTED BY MARCH 15

The new broadcasting approach I was discovering, of being more open and more vulnerable, was giving me back the confidence and the mojo that had been missing. After leaving the political editor role, I'd been struggling. But thanks to those stories and slots on *The Project* when I spoke from the heart and revealed this new Paddy, I felt things were getting back on track.

Not quite, though. Truth be told, the job as national correspondent was proving difficult. I felt like the role just didn't fit anywhere. I was supposed to be a senior journalist breaking my own stories and covering the important yarns, but it often seemed the bosses didn't know what to do with me, or didn't want to bother me. Or maybe they'd forgotten about me? It really messed with my head.

That was particularly the case on March 15, 2019. I was in Wellington driving back to the newsroom after filming something when I heard on the radio just after 1 p.m. that there'd been a shooting at a mosque in Christchurch. It was obviously a big story even on those details alone — but the question was, how big? On the motorway, I started ringing the bosses to ask if I should go. There was limited information, and the early stages of big breaking news can be chaotic with so many decisions to be made and so many moving parts. I couldn't get hold of anyone, and no one was ringing me. My worries about the national-correspondent role were magnified.

So I just made a decision myself. I said to the camera operator who was driving, 'Fuck it, bro. Take me to the airport. I'm just gonna go down myself and sort this out later.' At the airport, I booked onto the first flight to Christchurch, confident I could make it in time to help with the 6 p.m. news coverage. I still wasn't clear on what had happened — no one was — but I was pleased to be on the plane. Then, we sat there on the runway. I was looking at the time, wondering what was happening and why the hell we hadn't taken off. Then cop after cop started filing onboard. They were going to Christchurch, too, and the plane had been held up for them. This was very big.

The Civil Aviation Authority would be annoyed with me saying this, but I didn't turn my phone off as we headed down the runway and I used it in the air to find out as much as I could. There had been attacks at two mosques, Al Noor and Linwood, by a terrorist who'd premeditated the whole act, even live-streaming it and sending out a manifesto. As we flew to Christchurch, I found the manifesto on Twitter and read it before we landed. Reading the killer's hate-filled document brought another devastating realisation — this was a white-supremacist attack.

That triggered something really big for me, but I didn't have time to think about it.

This was an absolutely massive story, the biggest I would cover in New Zealand. I knew I'd made the right call, and the bosses were glad I'd got myself there. As soon as I landed I was sent to one of the high schools to go live into the 6 p.m. bulletin reporting on the locked-down students. Then I sped over to Deans Avenue to a cordon not far from the Al Noor mosque. *The Project* was due to come on at 7 p.m. but they were scrambling around with no one on the ground. I offered to help, and ended up reporting live from the cordon from 7 p.m. until midnight, because the coverage just kept rolling as the country took in what had happened.

Throughout the night, it was mostly just me and a camera operator. Usually in those situations you'd have a producer finding people to interview, but because there was so much going on and we were all spread so thin, we didn't have anyone. So when I wasn't on air, I'd be off trying to find people who were happy to go live on TV. During a short break, I went to a house near the mosque and saw through the ranch slider that the guy was watching TV3. I asked if he'd seen anything and he told me he had. 'Come with me,' I said, and pretty much grabbed him out of his lounge to be interviewed. I didn't even know what he'd witnessed until we were live; it was edgy stuff. He'd come face to face with the terrorist but just been left alive — he was a non-Muslim Pākehā. That lodged in my head: *Fuck, he didn't want to kill white people.* That may be obvious now, but at the time everything was happening so fast and I'd had no time to think, and his words really hit me.

Late in the night, it was announced that 40 people were dead. About that time, an Iraqi couple approached me. The wife said her son was missing and wanted to know if we could ask if anyone knew anything about him. I asked if she wanted to come on TV to make the appeal for information herself. So she and her husband stepped up. Everything was happening so quickly and I wasn't thinking things through properly. I told her on live TV that the latest information was that 40 people were dead. She had absolutely no idea. I immediately thought, *I've made a really big mistake here.* She burst into tears. A lot of people watching were angry and made complaints. And they were right.

That was my first interaction with the family of a March 15 victim. And it was far from ideal. I've been haunted by some things from March 15, including that moment. But it led to a beautiful connection with the family, including mum Janna Ezat, after I sought them out afterwards to apologise and put things right. I became friends with them and helped tell the story of their son, Hussein Al-Umari, as they fought for recognition of the heroic role he played that day. When the terrorist was shooting inside Al Noor and people started diving and running for cover, Hussein charged straight towards him in an attempt to stop him.

In the days after the attack, I was like a reporter possessed, zoned in and focused. There was a strange moment for me when the prime minister, Jacinda Ardern, showed up. I saw the minivan with the Press Gallery contingent travelling with her drive past. For ten years, I'd been in that van. But as I stood with victims' families, I knew I was in the right place for me now, outside of the political bubble, on the ground with the people. It wasn't anything against the journos in the van, it was more a realisation that this was the kind of mahi I was meant to do.

I was outside the mosque interviewing people when a young Somali guy called Abdi walked up to me as we were filming. He started talking while the camera was going, saying he'd been at the Friday prayers. He told me his younger brother, Mucad Ibrahim, had been killed. Abdi had taken Mucad to prayers with him and was with him when the shooting started. 'Everybody started running and I just lost the boy. He was three years old.'

Until that point, we hadn't heard of anyone so young being killed. We knew a lot of people had been killed, but a three-year-old? I forgot I was a journo, and started crying. I reached out to him and said, 'I'm sorry.' I just didn't know what else to say. I'd covered plenty of stories where I'd seen evil things, but it was at that moment when I learnt a three-year-old had been killed that I realised this was next-level evil. That interview broke me, and has always haunted me as well, mainly just thinking of little Mucad, and remembering Abdi's eyes when he said, 'I just lost the boy.' I referred to Mucad as my 'little Kiwi brother' in one of my reports, and it made me determined to do right by the victims and their families.

I also remember being on my own walking through the Botanic Gardens near the mosque when I saw a guy who looked lost and didn't seem well. I asked if he was okay and if there was anything I could do to help. He said his name was Mohammad — there were a few Mohammads associated with the mosques — and that he'd been there when the terrorist came in, and his friends were killed. I comforted him and helped him find his way to where some other victims were gathering. I hadn't even thought about interviewing him or asking for his story or number — this was not about being a journalist; I was just trying to help the guy out.

A couple of days later, there was a memorial service and I saw Mohammad again. He was with his family and he seemed a lot better. 'Do you remember me?' I asked. 'Yes, this is my wife and children.' It was good to see him with his family and a lot more settled.

Ten days after the attacks, the Al Noor mosque had been revamped, with a deep clean and new paint and carpet. The community was preparing to return and Hamish Clark, who was the *Newshub* bureau chief in Christchurch, asked if I could find out if we were allowed inside. He'd famously filmed inside the Christchurch Cathedral soon after the 2011 earthquake. I said I'd give it a nudge but I didn't fancy our chances.

I had a list of names of elders and senior members, some of whom had founded the mosque. As was often the way, people passed me on to someone else, and suggested other names. Eventually someone passed me a number for a guy, another Mohammad, who might be able to help, but warned: 'He's having a few problems so he may not talk, but give him a try.' I wasn't feeling confident, but I rang up and said I was Patrick Gower from *Newshub* and that I was sorry to trouble him. He was immediately friendly. I explained I wanted to find out if we could come inside the mosque to film and if he knew how I could go about it. 'Oh, yes — meet me at the mosque in half an hour.'

I was standing outside the mosque on Deans Avenue, not sure who I was looking for, when Mohammad from the Botanic Gardens walked up and smiled. 'Hello, are you ready to go inside?' Yes, he was the guy I had spoken to on the phone — I hadn't realised, but he'd made the connection. When I'd met him the two previous times, I had no idea he was one of the founders of the mosque, and I'd never asked — I'd only ever dealt with him as someone I needed to make sure was okay.

I suddenly understood at a deeper level why he was so upset — as a founder of the mosque, he'd built this place of worship for people to pray in and come together. And on that day it had been used for evil. We stood in the mosque together and filmed as he showed me where he was kneeling in prayer that day, took me through what the terrorist did, and told me what he'd witnessed. It was surreal to be inside the mosque, and to see and hear what had happened from my new friend. As he knelt for prayer I realised I was the first journalist inside the mosque. I knew that came with a responsibility. I suddenly had a new purpose.

”

I felt empathy for the families of the mosque attacks in a personal way. I look at people coming from other countries to New Zealand, and I see my own family. Everyone should be entitled to that Kiwi dream, no matter what colour you are. What's the difference whether you come from Ireland or Iraq or Pakistan? It's the same dream. You just want to create something better for your kids and grandkids, which is what my family did — but the Muslim community faced racism and discrimination. I'd sit down with victims' families and think, *This is what my family was like except we're white.* I can't stand racism; in my view if you're a Kiwi, you're a Kiwi, no matter the colour of your skin.

There was something else that haunted me the whole time

I was covering March 15, an episode that had happened a few months before, and which I'd had that sinking feeling about when I read the terrorist's manifesto on the plane. It was shameful — undoubtedly the biggest fuck-up of my career; a mistake that gave a platform to far-right activists whose views likely helped build the terrorist's racist ideology.

In 2018, Canadian so-called free-speech advocates Stefan Molyneux and Lauren Southern came to New Zealand. They were due to speak in Auckland but venues were cancelled, amid protest and counter-protest. Before they arrived, they'd been in Australia mocking Aboriginal culture and tearing down multiculturalism and Islam. They were notorious for their pseudo-scientific racial views. In other words, they were big trouble, and I should've known better than to do what I did.

I was assigned to the story and, after covering the ruckus outside one of the venues that had pulled out, I had enough for the 6 p.m. bulletin. I should have left it there. Instead, I started talking to their manager about interviewing them. One thing led to another, and next thing they were on their way into the newsroom. What was worse, I'd agreed to live-stream it online. I wasn't prepared. I hadn't watched anything about them, I knew very little about them, and I didn't know much about white supremacy. Right from the time they arrived, there was a gloomy feeling. From the moment we went live, I knew I was in trouble. They constantly flipped things around and made me look like a bystander rather than an interviewer. I considered stopping the interview, but thought that might look bad, too. So I kind of froze, which was actually even worse.

I needed something to get me out of it, but there was no help on the way. The News Gods said, 'You're on your own on this one, pal.' And Paddy Luck had well and truly run out.

I hadn't researched, I wasn't in the zone, and I was against two absolute pros who knew what they were out to do — which was to rip me to pieces and create viral content for their global YouTube channels. They had a plan and I didn't. They were professional arguers and I was never going to get any decent answers from them. Instead I let them speak their pseudo-scientific racial views. I finally found a way to end it, and actually physically hung my head in shame. They'd humiliated me.

A lot of my colleagues were embarrassed and annoyed. One of the most painful things was finding out that Mike McRoberts didn't think they should have been on TV, let alone live, and that the whole thing was a fuck-up. I really looked up to Mike, so to find that out was gutting. I'd let a lot of people down.

Molyneux and Southern got their wish in that it went viral and there were lots of clips of me being 'wrecked and destroyed'. It didn't end there — I was bombarded by their supporters from around the world constantly calling me a loser, going into any strand on my social media and attacking me. I've played it back in my head lots of times, and I should have walked off to end the interview, refusing to platform their views. I've also worked out why I did the interview in the first place: because of ego. I wanted to be the big man and interview these two controversial characters. I let my big ego get in the way and I paid the price.

When I read the Christchurch terrorist's manifesto, and the more I learnt about him, the more I realised, *I bet he was a fan of Molyneux and Southern and I wonder if he watched the interview.* The terrorist was living in New Zealand at the time of their visit.

He hung out in the same online forums their supporters did, he was radicalised by YouTube, and when the Royal Commission of Inquiry into the attacks came out it was revealed he'd donated to Molyneux's YouTube channel. I believe it was highly likely the terrorist saw my interview with Southern and Molyneux, and if he did there was no doubt I was a laughing stock for him. I've got to own that.

"

It was a lesson that our mistakes can have huge consequences, that things we do in the media can have ramifications we don't realise. I tried to put things right with investigations into white supremacy and online hate. Then in July 2021, I got a secretive approach that I can't detail to protect the source, but let's just say it was like something out of Hollywood — because it was from Hollywood. There were some crazy clandestine scenes, a whistleblower and suddenly a script for a movie about March 15 called *They Are Us* fell off the back of a truck and ended up in my lap. The first seventeen pages were a horrible recreation of the shooting.

I asked Salwa Mohamad, whose husband Khaled and son Hamza were killed, if she wanted to read the script. She did, and she told me it was worse than the terrorist's livestream. I promised to do everything I could to help her stop it and I broke the story. Three weeks later, Kiwi director Andrew Niccol announced the movie would be stopped. I felt that I had given something back to the victims of March 15.

19.
THE TRIKAFTA MIRACLE

When you're on the telly you become public property. It didn't take long for people to start recognising me, and that has increased all the time, especially after 'This is the Fucking News' blew up. I'm all good with it — although I would say I cannot stand the term 'famous'. I hate being called famous, or being thought of as famous.

Back in my early political reporter days, when people saw me, you could see them thinking, *Oh, there's that kooky guy who does politics*; as I improved as a political editor, they'd say to me, 'Keep giving the bastards shit, Patrick. I just love it — give them shit.'

So I was used to people coming up to me. But after leaving politics and sharing more about myself, I noticed more people were calling me Paddy instead of Patrick and talking about their own personal experiences or thanking me for something I'd said. I was doing yarns with a bit more purpose behind them, and people were noticing. The engagement was much more meaningful; they'd talk to me as if they knew me, and I was feeling a much deeper connection with Kiwis. I was travelling a lot up and down the country for work and meeting lots of people every day, and I always stopped and talked if I could. It meant I had my own 'vibe-o-meter' on what mattered to Kiwis — like hundreds of little focus groups. People were really open.

It can get confusing when I meet people. Sometimes they act like they know me — because they feel as if they do, from their TV screens. But I've met so many people that now I can never be sure, especially when they're so friendly — *Maybe I do know them from somewhere?* So I always keep the conversation going, trying to look for clues, because I don't want to embarrass them if I do know them and I've just forgotten. My brain will be scrambling, trying to find a name or something, and then, bang: *Oh, that's right, that's so-and-so who was my flatmate's friend at university.* Or: *I remember now — I met him at Oktoberfest.* So, since I don't want to snub anyone, I'll have long conversations with complete strangers until I feel reassured I don't actually know them.

Anyway, once I started opening up, people would stop me and say, 'Hey Paddy, I'm sorry, I know you're busy' — 99.9 per cent of Kiwis are incredibly polite — 'but I just wanted to say I love what you said about bullying.' Or 'I just wanted to say that I've struggled as a workaholic, too.' It feels amazing when people stop me just to say thanks for something I have said or some story I've done. It makes it all worthwhile, and I really make an effort to thank people for their work because I know how good it feels.

There is one group that always tracks me down and stops me wherever I am — people with cystic fibrosis and their families.

It all started with a random email, full of spelling mistakes and virtually no capital letters, which is almost always a bad sign. But this email was signed by Professor Sir Bob Elliott. It said he'd been researching cystic fibrosis and there was now a drug that worked to fix it, and he knew a girl who was going to die without it.

I knew a little bit about Sir Bob, mainly that he was a pioneer of child-health research responsible for an array of breakthroughs, including using the heel-prick test on babies to identify cystic fibrosis at birth. Was this email really from him?

It was a Thursday night and I didn't have much on, so I picked up the phone and rang him. Quickly I realised, yes, it was the real Sir Bob. He told me about the girl he'd written about, Bella Powell, and how he'd been working with her since she was young as part of his cystic fibrosis research. He explained there was now a drug produced overseas, and from the work he'd done he could see that it would keep Bella — and others like her — alive.

This was one hell of a yarn. So I started talking about flying from Wellington to see him in Auckland, maybe even the next day. Sir Bob paused, then said, 'I'll be honest with you, I'm not very well at the moment.' I didn't need to know the details but the poorly written email made a little more sense. 'Oh, do you want to get your wife on the phone and I'll try to figure something out with her? I don't want to put any pressure on you.' He then lowered his voice and whispered: 'We won't be telling Betsy because she won't let me do it.' After another pause, he said, 'I'll see you tomorrow.' I went around to his house in Remuera and the first thing I noticed was that he was walking very slowly and looked extremely sick. 'Are you OK, Sir Bob?' I asked him.

Instead of getting any fancy medical terms, he simply said,

'I'm on my way out.' He had cancer, and only weeks to live.

He sat in his armchair, a shrunken frame inside his suit, his voice raspy. But there was no denying his mana, and the force of his message. He explained that while his work on cystic fibrosis had helped extend the life expectancy of patients from seven to ten years old to about 40, he had always searched for more gains. Now he'd seen something, a drug called Trikafta, made by an American company called Vertex Pharmaceuticals. While it couldn't cure cystic fibrosis, it could stop the worst of it and give people a longer, better life. Sir Bob even called it a 'miracle drug'. But the problem was it cost about $500,000 for a year's supply. He ripped into how, in his opinion, it was unethical for the drug to cost that much, and how Pharmac, the government's drug-buying agency, needed to move quickly and subsidise it to save lives.

Sir Bob had a two-pronged plan. Part one was to save Bella's life. He knew she was going to die without Trikafta, so he paid $100,000 of his own money to buy her a course of the drug to give her a chance. I'll never forget what he said: 'Money doesn't matter to me, I'm a medical guy, I don't care. I'm interested in saving lives.'

Part two was getting the story out. I'd realised while talking to him that he didn't really know who I was. He obviously watched TV One. It turned out a priest had recommended to him that I might be the person who could do the job. 'I'm buying the drug for Bella because when I'm gone, I want people to see the results in a person, and I want the message to get out that people need this drug.' He had thought it all through.

I felt a sense of responsibility — Sir Bob had just given me the task of completing his last wish. The more he spoke, the more I was drawn in. He'd worked his whole life to help other people, to save lives. And he was expecting me to help him help all the cystic fibrosis patients in New Zealand. I was in. At the end, I went over to his armchair, knelt down, shook his hand gently, and told him: 'I know what you're trying to do and you've come to the right guy.' I never saw Sir Bob again. He died three weeks later.

"

Straight after seeing Sir Bob, we went to the North Shore to meet Bella. She held the pills and said: 'These are a miracle. I was going to die and now I'm going to live.'

'How long did they take to work?' I asked.

'One day,' she replied.

'What?'

'One day.'

Problem was, Bella would die as soon as she stopped taking the pills.

I worked on the story all weekend and we put it out on the Sunday night. There was a public appeal and people quickly donated Bella money to get her a year's worth of the drug. Cystic fibrosis and Trikafta were put front and centre. Until then, I had no idea there were 500 people dealing with this disorder — and I admit that at the start I wasn't even sure what it was, how it damaged people's lungs until it sucked them out of life. I realised the cystic fibrosis community felt unseen and forgotten. So I brought it up with the leaders in the 2020 election debate, and straight afterwards I remember one dad wrote to me thanking me for even saying the words 'cystic fibrosis' on such a big platform. His son had died but he wanted Trikafta funded so other parents wouldn't have to go through what they did. He wrote how he could still hear his son's cough. I still cry every time I think of his letter.

Still, the issue lagged a bit, and I moved on to other stories. A few months later I got a call from a patient, Ed Lee, and his wife, KP. He was on the drug because his family was fortunate to have enough money, but the couple was evangelical about making it affordable for others. Ed was another miracle story, literally running around Oriental Parade when he had previously struggled to breathe. They were on a mission to get the drug funded; Ed had even worked out a cost–benefit analysis for the taxpayer.

I'd gone into the meeting a little unsure about what more I could do. But at one point KP looked straight at me, her eyes brimming with tears. She told me she thought she'd be widowed at 31, but Trikafta meant she had Ed back, and they could start a proper life.

It was like KP had laser-beams in her eyes that compelled me to do something more, to get going again. I was back in. My friend Shannon Redstall, a brilliant journalist, started helping, and we went really hard with a series of stories that ended with a guy called Izaeah Twose who had a few pills left and went on camera saying he was probably going to die. A supply of Trikafta was gifted to him anonymously, days later.

The thing that really struck me about cystic fibrosis was the way everybody died young. It was all young people who'd been given a death sentence. They could never have any dreams, because they weren't going to live. It was just so cruel. The cystic fibrosis community started rising up, which was awesome, but it was taking so long. I'd meet all these cystic fibrosis mums, they all had the same worry and desperation in their eyes. They were used to waiting, because they spent so much time in hospitals. They'd all decided they weren't going to wait anymore. It was powerful to see.

Meanwhile, I started getting really frustrated, too, wondering why, as a country, we just couldn't seem to get shit done anymore. There were people dying, there was a drug that could let them live, and we couldn't just tick the boxes and get it sorted. It was going on and on, there were people with cystic fibrosis moving overseas because it was funded elsewhere — it just seemed so ridiculous.

Then I was standing at the chemist one day, waiting for a prescription of dandruff shampoo, when the phone rang. It was Pharmac telling me they were about to make an announcement that Trikafta was going to be funded. I started crying and had to sit down because I was so overwhelmed. The people in the pharmacy checked on me but I explained they were tears of joy. So many lives would be saved. Faces just came flashing back to me of all the cystic fibrosis families I'd met, all the worried mums who weren't going to have to worry anymore.

I went back to see Sir Bob's wife, Lady Betsy, and his kids and grandkids, for a story about the announcement. We filmed in the lounge where I'd interviewed him, where I'd made that promise to him, and I said to myself, *I told you I'd help.*

”

I loved working with purpose, doing stories that mattered to me, stories that were making a difference. I was finally breaking free of politics. But there was still a hangover from my time in the gallery: my mental health and drinking were way off track. And I was still doing some crazy, messy stuff. I was invited to be part of a show at a Wellington theatre where I was to be interviewed by comedian Robbie Nicol playing the satirical news-presenter character from his show *White Man Behind a Desk.* I hoed into the 7 per cent craft beers beforehand, took a beer with me on stage that I sculled, then got handed another one and downed that, too. I was pissed. Which perhaps explained what happened next.

I had a real beer buzz on, and I couldn't resist playing to the audience. There was a camera recording everything — something I should have clocked, but didn't. The whole slurring train wreck of an 'interview' ended up on YouTube. Robbie asked me questions about other news personalities. I dissed Sean Plunket, which the leftie Wellington crowd loved, so it just provoked me further. Mike Hosking — who I had never met and I actually really liked listening to — was next: I called him an 'absolute fucking disgrace'. I went after Duncan Garner, calling him an embarrassment. Even Mike McRoberts wasn't safe: I claimed he had a *3News* tattoo on his butt. I said I'd been a climate denier. It was just an outrageous bunch of bullshit for a laugh.

But they weren't laughing at work. The bosses wanted me to apologise to Duncan, get in contact and say sorry. I don't think I ever did, but I'll say sorry now. And I don't know Mike Hosking, but I should apologise to him, too, because I was a complete dickhead. The truth was, the only disgrace was me. The truth was, I was still in the spiral I thought would end when I left the gallery. The truth was, I was letting things get me down, and I just kept going down and down ever further.

The ongoing problems with my eyes, for instance, really kicked my arse. I catastrophised what was going on and became convinced I'd go blind, even though I'd been assured that the glaucoma treatment and the surgeries for the detached retinas had worked. I lost all my confidence at work.

There was one time, in the months after my second retina went again and I thought I'd gone blind, that I lied to my bosses about what was going on because I was scared. I'd been off *The Project* for a few months recovering, but I was due to return. I wasn't sure whether my eyes would be good enough for the autocue or to engage with the room — obviously big parts of being a presenter on a live TV show. Rather than just say what was going on, I rang the boss, Sarah Bristow, and said I didn't feel well and that maybe I had Covid. Sarah must have suspected something because she rang back and pressed me: 'Is it your eyes? Is there still something wrong with your eyes?' I lied again, assuring her my eyes were perfectly fine and I was just not feeling well. In truth, I couldn't see properly yet, and was terrified of not being able to perform at the level I needed to — and that I might never be able to again.

”

All of this came on top of Covid. There wasn't a lot for me to do. Early on, we made a documentary about the first lockdown — which got me around a deserted New Zealand, even seeing a scientist in a secure laboratory, handling one of the only samples of the disease in the country at that time. In 2021, I was asked to be involved with the 'Vaxathon', a government effort to increase the vaccination numbers.

It was a big decision but I decided to get off the journalistic fence and encourage people to get the jab. Eight hours and a bit of dancing on live TV later, I had the nickname 'Matua Paddy G'. Being involved in that broadcast, and later an undercover investigation about a Christchurch doctor giving away false vaccine exemptions, made a lot of vaccine-hesitant people hate me. It was a tense time, with the occupation of Parliament soon after, too. A lot of the occupiers wanted me to come down, but I stayed away and didn't get involved in any way — even though it was a huge story happening just down the road from me.

I'm still pro-vaccine, but I'm now prepared to admit that the voices of people who didn't want to take it were dismissed too strongly at times. It came home to me when I did a story about a pro-vaccine guy who'd suffered side effects from the jab and nearly died, but felt boxed out and ostracised by his family and society because he was complaining. It was a lesson that it is always important to try to listen to people, even if it feels hard.

”

The reality was, for nearly two years, my work almost completely dried up, especially during the lockdowns. I was just expected to sit at home because they only had a skeleton crew in the office. I'd never been good with technology so working from home was hopeless for me. I'd sometimes go days without even hearing from work. The biggest story of our generation was playing out and I wasn't reporting on it. I did not handle that well.

I couldn't get out of bed. I'd doom-scroll on my phone for hours. And I'd drink, taking pride in the overflowing recycling bin, chocka full of craft-beer empties, empty bottles of red and a gin bottle or two for good measure. It all just contributed to ripping the guts out of me.

People would message me and say, 'Just enjoy the sunshine.' I felt like saying to them: 'Don't fucking tell me to enjoy the sunshine, I don't want to enjoy the fucking sunshine.' I eventually realised what was going on. I remembered how years earlier the sun had made me mad before, when I used to watch it just out of reach on the deck of that dingy flat in Herne Bay.

I was depressed again.

20.
WEED, DRUGS AND BOOZE

Aside from 'This is the Fucking News', there is another moment Kiwis really know me for: smoking weed on TV. It all started when I was walking across the car park at work in Auckland one day — and I've got Paul Henry to thank for it. TV3's building in Flower Street, Auckland, was not the flashest place: it was an old converted dairy factory. And at the time the company was so broke it was renting out the car parks to punters — employees had to park on the street. It's not where you'd expect a career-changing moment to strike. But there I was when I bumped into Szusty, Andrew Szusterman, the boss of all of TV3's big shows. He stopped me, just pointed, and said: 'Cannabis.'

'Um,' I replied. 'What about it?'

'How do you feel about it?'

It was a strange question for one of the bosses to ask. I rambled through an answer that encompassed the facts: that like many Kiwis I'd smoked it, but I wasn't a stoner; that I didn't use it much at all anymore; that I'd once found my Old Man's weed tin in the back of the liquor cabinet; and that I didn't care enough to have a view on whether it should be legal or not.

Szusty said: 'What would you think about making a documentary about cannabis?' He'd seen a piece on cocaine by British chef Gordon Ramsay and it made him think it was time for a cannabis documentary — bearing in mind there was going to be a referendum about legalisation at the coming election.

'Oh, yeah,' I said. 'Could be keen, but there's one condition — I'd want to do it with my mate Justin Hawkes.'

Justin and I had been to university at Victoria together, I'd gone off to journalism and he'd gone to film school. He'd since moved on to directing TV, including David Farrier's Netflix hit, *Dark Tourist*. For twenty years, we'd dreamt about doing a documentary together — we'd even pitched an idea about a Donald Trump doco to TV3, but got turned down because the bosses didn't think he'd become president. Here was a chance to work together. 'Yep, sure, I like Justin,' said Szusty.

I later found out Paul Henry had just turned Szusty down for the job. Which is why the idea was in his head when he'd seen me in the car park. Funny the way that opportunity comes knocking — next minute, Justin was on board, it was funded by New Zealand on Air, and the project was all go. I was making a documentary: *Patrick Gower: On Weed.*

Initially, I wasn't that into the topic, I just wanted to make a doco. But from the first day that news of the doco became public, people started contacting me asking how they could help, mainly as my personal tester. Or inviting me to come to see the best weed in New Zealand, with the messages coming from up and down the motu. Until then, I'd only thought of weed as a recreational drug, but there were a lot of people wanting to talk about medicinal weed as well.

Justin did a bunch of research, and called me in for a meeting. He mapped out the documentary, which would show everything from the criminal underworld to places in the world where it was legal. I found myself saying, 'We're going to do what?' And then: 'You sure we can get away with it?' And: 'Will they let us do that?' Then: 'I might end up getting fired if we do that.' He finished his spiel and I thought: *I knew Justin was good, but this documentary is going to be the shit!*

Day one of the shoot was with a bearded hippie who called himself Gandalf, in Northland. He pulled out an exercise book listing all his medicinal-weed customers around the country, with copious notes on their conditions and what doses worked. Gandalf opened one page and there in his tidy handwriting was a woman with lung cancer. I stopped him. That's what Mum had died of. 'Lung cancer — I know a lot about that. What's the story here?' He told me about this woman who was terminal and had been enduring a lot of pain and the cannabis was really helping her deal with it. As he explained, I had a moment: even though I'd smoked weed myself, while I sat there watching my Old Lady go through so much pain, it had never occurred to me that cannabis could help her. I had no idea that it could be dispensed in drops, that she wouldn't even have had to smoke it. On day one of filming, Gandalf, an ageing hippy who told me he hadn't worn undies for 40 years, was giving me a lesson. My journey into the world of weed had begun.

Justin had been listening to podcasts where people interviewed their parents and he came up with the idea of me interviewing Dad about Mum's death. Documentary-making could be a bit bizarre at the best of times — an intimate space, yet surrounded by multiple cameras, microphones on booms, and lights. As we sat down together, about to start, it dawned on me: *Fuck — I've never actually spoken with Dad about Mum dying.* About as much as we'd ever said to each other was the morning after her funeral when we woke up in the lounge and he said, 'She's gone, mate. She's gone.' Which was about as Kiwi male as it gets.

And here we were, about to kōrero with cameras rolling. I started with some basic questions to start us off gently, but it was all too heavy and no amount of gently-gently was going to work. Soon the two of us burst into tears. It was such a heavy conversation to have, let alone on a documentary set. Even though the situation had been contrived, we opened up in a way we never had. We talked about how, while both of us could've got our hands on some cannabis for Mum, it just never occurred to us. Instead we'd all trundled off to the chemist for those car seats full of bags of pills, while Mum suffered in pain. The stigma around cannabis and its absence from the discussion in mainstream medicine had blinded us to a choice we should've considered.

It was cathartic, and it was the first time I'd bawled my eyes out on camera. There had been a few small tears before — during the March 15 coverage, and even when we filmed with Gandalf. But from hereon in, the tears rolled so much during the documentary shoot that Justin started calling me 'Mr Weepy'.

We headed to America, where cannabis was legal in some states, and Justin had an idea of me using weed myself to deal with my anxiety and stress. At work, the whole documentary had put the shits up the more conservative news bosses from the get-go. The idea of me smoking weed on screen sent them into panic stations, with huge concerns about reputational damage. But it was legal in Colorado where we were heading to film, so they agreed to me doing it as long as I got a cannabis prescription from a doctor.

The kindly doctor gave me the prescription with extreme ease; he even pulled out a vape for me to do it then and there. My anxiety and stress disappeared immediately and the Colorado snow suddenly became really interesting to look at. In California, a Kiwi woman was marketing cannabis tea as an alternative to wine. Justin had the idea of me going along to a taste test — perfectly legal in California, but outside what the bosses had agreed. I made the decision to film first and ask permission later, and we rolled up to a fancy house in the California hills. I sipped tea with these very glamorous women and, after my first cup kicked in, pulled the horn of an imaginary train and said, 'Choo, choo.' It was absolutely fucking hilarious TV. I'd managed to get stoned on TV not once but twice.

The documentary, which rolled out in two parts, turned out to be a massive hit. It meant a few things: firstly, I'd be offered weed everywhere I went (thanks, but no thanks). It also meant Justin and I got the green light to do a bunch more documentaries. And it started me on a bigger journey learning about drugs and addiction. Justin and I ended up making documentaries about P, methamphetamine — the drug that was behind so many of those violent crimes I'd reported on back in the day at the *Herald* — and then one on a range of other drugs, such as MDMA and mushrooms, looking at drug laws.

I started out very judgemental about people with addictions — I thought they were weak, and should just give up. I came to see that addicts needed help, that addiction was really a disease that needed to be treated. That turn-around was most evident in my view towards P — I realised that, as a country, we'd stuffed up by arresting users. Helping addicts to get off the drug is the only way we can get on top of it. Putting users in jail is useless; they need to be in the health system. Without helping them, all we are doing is creating demand for the drug, a market of addicts for the gangs to supply. We should still be going after the dealers and suppliers but, if we ever want to fix the meth problem, we have to focus on helping people get off it.

When it comes to cannabis, after all my research I now view it as a relatively harmless recreational drug that nobody should be arrested for. I believe it should be decriminalised for personal use for the simple reason cops have better things to do. I don't think it should be fully legal in shops, but there's a middle path that suits the Kiwi weed scene — let people grow enough for themselves and their mates, and only punish those who commercialise it or deal to kids. As for legal medicinal cannabis, it's still hard to get because there's so much red tape. It's just another example of New Zealand not being able to get shit done, and people suffering because of it.

With MDMA, there's no point in turning a blind eye to how popular this is now. Under the current law, Rhythm and Vines is technically the country's biggest criminal gathering every year, not that anybody going, or their parents, think of it that way. With my documentary work, I've come to believe small amounts of MDMA should be decriminalised, too. It's better that people focus on getting it tested to be safe. We need to relax laws around LSD and mushrooms as well, which were dragged into America's 'War on Drugs' in the 1960s but actually have amazing mental-health treatment possibilities, yet their illegal status means scientists find it hard to do the research to properly find out.

I'm often asked my views on cigarettes and vaping, which I've done a *Patrick Gower: On Vaping* doco about. I think cigarettes should be heavily controlled, as close to a ban as possible. And sure, vaping can help cigarette smokers quit, but that's all it should be used for. The widespread availability of vapes for our young people is one of the stupidest things New Zealand has ever done. It's given a nicotine addiction to a whole new generation.

I have come to a very liberal view on drug laws, and I know this may seem controversial to some people. But it is all based on science and reality, and I've decided I can provoke some debate when it comes to drug reform, by making people think. We have things completely back to front: criminalising addicts of dangerous drugs who need help, and criminalising people who choose to use drugs that cause limited harm like weed and MDMA, whereas as a society we encourage the use of another, far more harmful drug. Which was exactly what was wrecking my own life — booze.

”

During the filming for the weed doco, plenty of people said, 'What about booze? It's just the worst and yet it's legal.' But I wasn't interested in any idea that alcohol was dangerous. It wasn't like we were avoiding the topic — we always knew we'd eventually get to alcohol as a subject for the *Patrick Gower: On . . .* series. I just never saw it in the same context as an 'actual' drug.

The format of the documentary series always included a personal aspect, so as we got underway with *Patrick Gower: On Booze*, Justin was concocting scenes that involved me drinking or confronting my problem drinking. He'd seen me getting on the booze for about 25 years — we'd met in Piss Drinking 101 at uni — and then, as we filmed the series, I'd often be turning up to shoots hungover. That could get a bit awkward because, although we were friends, he was also the director, and he wasn't happy about having his presenter turn up in a less-than-ideal state.

As the Oversharer-in-Chief, it was always odds-on I'd spill my guts on camera about the problems drinking had caused me down the years. But Justin and I both envisioned an ending where I'd take everything I'd learnt and be like, 'Okay, cheers!' . . . and keep on drinking.

Early on we filmed with an addiction specialist and counsellor named Grant Foster, who talked to me about my drinking, and we recorded a session with Alcoholics Anonymous where I was an observer. In both cases, my attitude was *What is this bullshit?* The night before I went to AA, I'd had a massive bender, but as I sat there I thought, *These guys are alcoholics — that's not me.* With Grant, I was quite aggressive and pushed back a lot. It ended with him saying, 'Hey, why don't you give not-drinking a go for a while and just see how it goes?'

Justin and I had always planned that during the filming I'd stop drinking for a month to see if I lost weight or slept better or whatever — some bullshit like that. I was just so dismissive of the whole thing. So I said to Grant, 'Yeah, yeah. Sweet as, mate.' My plan was to get Christmas and New Year's Eve out of the way and have a dry January and then it would be done.

Before the break, though, we had a couple more scenes to film. The first involved me catching up with Corin Dann, who'd been the political editor at TVNZ when I was *Newshub*'s. We were competitors but we were also mates and often by 6.15 p.m., after our live crosses, we'd be drinking together at the Backbencher pub across the road from Parliament. More than once we got trolleyed. He was now host of RNZ's *Morning Report* and had backed off the booze after leaving the gallery — whereas I'd well and truly carried on.

Corin was reluctant to have a beer on camera, and was nervous about the whole idea. But we met in an empty pub and, for a couple of guys who'd been in front of cameras for years, we quickly forgot the crew was even there. We got deep and he told me he was worried about my drinking. I wasn't having it and I was really pushing back. Corin is very much a teddy-bear kind of person and I'd never seen him get riled before, but he got wound up about me not admitting I had a drinking problem. Sure, we were filming for TV, but this was real — a guy worried about his mate; and that mate — me — in total denial. There was one thing he said that got through: 'I can't see how this ends well.' The interview finished kind of awkwardly, but I noticed Corin gave me a really big hug as he left.

The crew packed up and Justin and I arranged to catch up later on when we were due to film at a student party. The idea was for me to turn up a bit tipsy, and I didn't want to lose the beer buzz I already had; so while the others had lunch — the sensible option — I went on a mini pub crawl, bouncing around a couple of bars and day-drinking with whoever I came across. Before I got to the flat, I stopped at a liquor store because I was meant to be filmed showing up with my own grog. I walked up to the counter with a dozen beers and the guy refused to serve me. I was too drunk. It was about three o'clock in the afternoon, I was supposed to be working, and I was too pissed to even get served. While it was a shock, I had quite a bit of booze on board and I had obviously overcooked the hāngī. So full credit to the guy for refusing me.

I had to ring Justin to get him to come and buy the beers then give them to me on the street corner like I was a sixteen-year-old back in the day. Even though I was slurring, we managed to film the scene in the student flat, a place that itself carried a few shameful memories for me. Back at university, I used to hang out in this particular flat a bit, and one night, drunk, I'd 'fire-trucked' a bed there — stood up and pissed everywhere, still half asleep and out of it.

After disgracing myself here again during the filming, I bundled myself into a taxi and blacked out.

Justin rang in the morning, making sure I was okay for that day's filming. We were due to record with Corin's wife, Lotta, who'd been very public about going sober. I was hungover again and couldn't remember much from the night before, but I wasn't going to let Justin know that. In the best passive-aggressive tone I could muster I said, 'Yeah, yeah, I'm fine, bro. Fine. Why wouldn't I be?'

As soon as the cameras started rolling, Lotta politely started getting stuck into me. She started with a viral TikTok of me sculling a bottle on Crate Day, saying their teenage kids thought it was lame. Next thing, Justin started feeding her questions — as the director, he always stayed out of it during the interviews, but from behind the camera he started giving Lotta ideas of things to put to me. If anything, he was supposed to be feeding me questions, not her. It suddenly felt more like an intervention than an interview. I couldn't imagine another documentary where the director gave the talent ammunition to take on the presenter. But Justin had become a double agent because, as my friend, he was worried.

I scraped out of there, ego bruised — and still incredibly hungover. Fellow drinkers would understand this: I was so hungover that I couldn't face the thought of having a drink. This was basically the only time when I'd turn down a drink — when I was too hungover. The toxins had reached such a point after a heavy month of partying and pre-Christmas socialising that my body was in revolt.

I was driving to New Plymouth to see the Old Man for Christmas so I had a lot of time to think. The words of Grant the psychologist, Justin, Lotta and Corin went around and around in my head — maybe they were right and this wouldn't end well.

Dad offered me a beer when I arrived but I declined, to his surprise. I woke up the next day, on the brink of Christmas and New Year's — the busiest drinking period of the year — and for some reason, deep within, I thought: *Do it now, PG — start your month off.* I don't know why, maybe it was the ongoing hangover, maybe it was to prove everyone wrong.

I immediately started having withdrawal effects. I felt sluggish, I felt introverted, I felt anxious. But I also started to see some upsides: on Christmas Day I liked to go to the beach for a swim, and would usually have to get someone else to drive. One year I even got a taxi. But for the first time ever, I could drive myself there, and it felt good to be in the Taranaki sea.

New Year's was looming as a challenge — for a binge drinker like me, that was like the drinking Olympics. Wherever I'd been in the world — in the snow with my cousins in Ireland, on the beach at Mount Maunganui, at a Shihad concert in Northland — New Year's was always like, 'Okay, now is your night to prove yourself again and win your annual medal.' It was like a biological imperative, my body-clock alarm going off on 31 December, time to go and get pissed.

I was desperately trying to ignore that impulse as I headed to a mate's house for a party, fortifying myself by buying every non-alcoholic drink I could to give myself as many options as possible. I walked around the back, with my booze-free stash, and I saw five mates perched on chilly bins stocked with cold piss, each with a beer in their hands. I just thought, *Oh, fuck. This is going to be hard.*

21.
PATRICK GOWER:
OFF BOOZE

Somehow, I managed to white-knuckle it through New Year's Eve. The next day, for the first time in three decades, I started the year without a hangover. I even went for a bike ride with a friend. It was one of the Wellington-on-a-good-day days as we spun around the bays and, honestly, the world couldn't have looked better. We stopped at a cafe in Houghton Bay and I know I would have looked like the biggest Middle-Aged Male In Lycra, self-satisfied with my coffee, but I just couldn't stop smiling; it felt awesome to be sober.

I sent Corin and Lotta a video message telling them I was having a break from drinking. I'd left their house a bit miffed and ruffled after that interview with Lotta and the confrontation with Corin the day before. I wanted to share with them what I'd done. I didn't know where this whole thing would take me yet. But it felt good.

The positive changes came quickly — I started having the most amazing, deep sleep, and realised I'd been sleeping like crap for years. After about two weeks a strange thing started happening. I woke up feeling hungover, especially on weekends. I was having phantom hangovers — my body and mind were so used to me getting pissed, it just expected to wake up feeling terrible. It was pretty freaky, and a frightening realisation that drinking had twisted some stuff up inside me. But the phantom hangover was always quickly followed by a surge of energy, the realisation I was feeling great for the day ahead. I felt incredible, which I learnt is what's known as the 'pink cloud' sensation when people give up drinking.

I started reading to find out what was happening. Previously I'd never read an article about sobriety — I didn't give a fuck about sobriety. I'd never even tried to moderate my drinking. Suddenly, I couldn't read enough. And I started to notice how much alcohol and talk of alcohol was all around me — New Zealand's booze culture.

By the time we started filming again, I hadn't had a drink for over a month. We went back to see the addiction specialist, Grant, who we'd filmed earlier. He probed away about why I drank. For the first time I started to think about it. And I said to him: 'I started drinking because I didn't like the way I looked. I had no self-confidence.' I can tell you, until that moment I'd never thought about that in my life. Finally, I had connected two of my demons.

It was a paradigm shift for me — once I figured that out, my relationship with booze just collapsed. Because by then, I'd already moved past all the self-confidence issues, my looks just weren't an issue for me. I thought, *I'm sorry, Paddy, but that is fucked, bro — you've got past the stuff about the looks, but you're still carrying this crutch of alcohol. Booze is holding you back and you don't need it anymore.* I decided life was for living, and I didn't want to waste it anymore.

I also came to another realisation: that moderation was never going to work. I knew myself, and I knew I would never be able to have just a couple. I knew I could never touch alcohol without putting myself at risk of it taking over my life again. The reality was, I was an alcoholic. For me, the only way out of it was to never touch a drink again in my life.

"

Justin was blown away. 'Where did all this come from?' In the space of a few weeks on the doco I'd gone from a wild drinking maniac, someone who got so drunk on the job they couldn't be served, to a self-confessed alcoholic, committed to a life of sobriety. Justin is a creative genius, and I owe him a lot on the work front, but he's a genius of a friend, too, because he helped change my life. We finished the doco and sent it to the bosses to have a look. There was only so much I could do to prepare them for what they were about to see.

My boss Sarah Bristow rang and just said: 'Wow, PG.' She asked if I was sure I wanted all of this out there. I knew some of what was filmed was humiliating, and I knew admitting being an alcoholic was a very loaded term. But I just thought, *You know what? Fuck it. No one talks about this in this country. This is really going to push some people's boundaries and get right up in the grate of some people. And a whole lot of people are going to feel like it's them.* So I hoped it would help people. I pushed go.

The night before it aired, I started having serious doubts. I went to bed hoping I'd feel better in the morning and woke up feeling worse. I was on *The AM Show* for a promo interview with Ryan Bridge and Melissa Chan-Green. I told them I had a problem with alcohol and I'd had it for a long time. Their faces dropped in shock. *Uh oh*, I thought. Had I done the right thing? I was crapping myself. But it was too late, everything was locked in.

As the doco started playing that night, I got swamped with messages — many from people saying they were going through some of the things I'd been through. The feedback was incredible, thousands of messages from people, so many saying 'That was me.' It was the strangest way to give up alcohol, to tell an entire country in one go. It led to some unusual encounters.

The Friday after it screened, I was MC-ing a plumbers' conference — which, like many big events, featured alcohol quite heavily. Beforehand, I came out from behind a curtain to have a yarn with the crowd. There was a typical Kiwi couple, her with a wine, him with a Heineken. The guy stared at me as if he'd seen a ghost. 'Paddy!'

'Yep, how are ya?'

He was lost for words, so I tried to get the small talk going. Then he blurted out: 'Do you want a beer, mate?', and tried to pass me the one he was drinking.

I had to laugh. 'No, mate, I'm all good, thank you.' His wife was horrified, and went a deep red with embarrassment — it turned out they'd watched the show together.

A year on, I was hosting a charity auction, and there was a painting of dawn rising on the Wellington coast. It spoke to me on so many levels — the bright colours depicting a coastline I'd ridden so many times; a reminder of morning and how great it felt to wake up clear-headed; and a new beginning. I was the auctioneer, but bought it myself to celebrate twelve months off booze.

So much had changed — physically and psychologically. My ambition and drive was back, big time. I could see things more optimistically, and I'd become very calm. But it was far from easy. I came to realise I was an outsider. I felt the pressure of a society where alcohol was normal, and therefore I was not. And I realised I'd been part of the problem.

After the documentary, Justin reminded me of a time a few years earlier when he was trying not to drink. Rather than support him, or even respect him, I'd put the hard word on him, and told him he was boring. 'Come on, bro. One beer — it won't hurt you.' Once he said it, I remembered, and it hurt me to realise I'd been that guy.

I'm careful to not preach too much about booze — each to their own, and all that. But for me, I've taken a lot of power back, and I have conquered one of my demons. For me, it's about choosing to be different — different to the way I was, and different to the society around me.

”

By now, I had well and truly become a 'personality'. I really noticed this at the Queen's funeral in 2022. During the live coverage, I was stationed outside Jacinda Ardern's hotel where a large crowd had gathered. They obviously thought a celebrity was inside. I thought they'd be disappointed when they found out it was just Ardern, but when she emerged they gave her a huge, approving roar. I was shocked and said 'Fuck! They do know her!', not realising I was already live on air. Yet again, my phone lit up with text messages, and I thought I'd wrecked the vibe of *Newshub*'s funeral coverage. To my surprise, everybody, including my boss Sarah Bristow, seemed to think it was hilarious; Sarah just said 'That's PG.'

I was ready for a new challenge. And at the end of 2022, it came. Something we don't like to talk about much, something I really hate admitting: sometimes the bosses have good ideas. I was called into the bosses' office and they opened a laptop that had a concept on it, something called *Paddy Gower Has Issues*. As much as I'd like to say it was me who came up with it, it was actually my friend Todd Symons, a creative genius I've been lucky to have in my corner. I was teamed up with Jon Bridges, another good friend and creative genius, and who I'd come to know from *The Project*. Jon and I headhunted the best in the TV business, such as gun producers Bridget Mills and Arun Jeram, and camera op John Fleming. We leaned on all the amazing people at TV3 behind the scenes, and pulled every lever we could. Jon had the brilliant idea of bringing in comedian Karen O'Leary for a consumer-rights segment that was like *Fair Go* on MDMA.

Getting *PGHI* up and running was a dream come true. Being honest, I'd dreamt of my own show but had never seen a way of it happening. The documentaries were something Justin created that I was part of, but it wasn't the same. Over the years, media speculation would come up from time to time about me taking over certain shows — but the stories were always wrong. I'd never been keen. But now, the time had come to do it my way. I'd made so many mistakes in my career, and I was getting a second chance. I'd given up drinking and began really working on myself as a person, really concentrating on using my skills and gifts. I was optimistic, I was working with purpose. I was a completely different person to when I was political editor.

I really wanted to be seen as a leader and someone who could hack the pressure. I wanted to feel in control, I wanted to be calm, to work with the bosses rather than fight with them, to have people enjoy working with me and respect me. I'd never been more driven in my life.

When we got the team together for the first time, Jon and I talked about the kaupapa of the show, what it would be about. We decided it would be manaakitanga, caring for others.

We launched in 2023, bringing important issues to the attention of New Zealanders. That sounds really dry and boring, but I felt it was my destiny. We challenged how reading was taught in schools, debated what should happen with feral cats, chased answers over the death of a little boy at a beach covered in forestry slash. Then we had Karen tackling the banks, supermarkets and politicians in her own special way. We produced seventeen shows and for me it felt like redemption — I'd left behind that persona of being a crackpot in the workplace, a political editor who shouted and broke phones, to someone who could have fun while getting the job done and helping others thrive.

From the beginning, too, it was important to me for *PGHI* to be a success for the business. It didn't have public funding, so it was backed by our owners, Warner Bros. Discovery. The show was reaching all its ratings targets for old-school television, the on-demand version, on the web and on social. But there was only one sign of commercial success I was focused on — getting the programme renewed. It sounded as if it would be, but as the months passed, and the health of WBD became gloomier, and the New Zealand economy became gloomier, it became difficult to tell what was going to happen. By the end of 2023, all we had was something that anyone who's been in this position will know is ultimately worthless: promises from bosses that were never written down. We kept waiting for a proper answer.

”

Before 2023 ended, though, I had one more job to do — filming in Antarctica. I was going with Justin to film a documentary on climate change, *Patrick Gower: On Ice*.

Because of the frantic year, in classic Paddy style, I was quite disorganised before we went. I'd missed every deadline on filling out the forms I was supposed to, and was in a rush getting my gear sorted. So rather than being excited checking in at Auckland Airport to make my way to Christchurch to fly to the ice, I was grumpy and dealing with first-world problems — how was I going to cope with my mistakenly purchased medium-sized Icebreaker thermal rather than a large?

So I was hardly the great Antarctic adventurer as we started our tour of the base. Not helping was that Justin and Dom Fryer, the director of photography on the shoot, always gave me grief for getting special treatment wherever we went. We were shown to the sleeping quarters, a six-person bunkroom. None of us was looking forward to this, but we had to do what we had to do, and at least we were all in this together. I went to put my gear down and the guy showing us around said, 'Hang on, Paddy, you're not in there, we've got another room for you.' The look on Justin and Dom's faces was priceless.

I was led to another wing where I was still going to have to share a room, but only with one person. It even had an ensuite, with a nice hot shower. When Justin and Dom came to check out my room, I didn't open the ensuite door and pretended it was a cupboard — there was no point demoralising them this early in the trip.

At dinner that first night, we sat with some scientists and Antarctic old hands, having a chow-down and a yarn about the things coming up. We were talking about all the things we'd like to do, and I was mulling over telling them about something I'd dreamt of — being on an iceberg watching a polar bear. Now, keep in mind I'd been in a rush to get down there — one minute I was finishing off filming *PGHI* and worrying about its future, and the next I was on the ice — so I hadn't done all the research and reading I should have. One of the scientists piped up: 'It's amazing how many people come down here thinking they're going to see a polar bear.' Fortunately, some instinct kicked in and I resisted the urge to say, 'Why can't they see a polar bear?' I let him talk for a bit longer, and he revealed that polar bears only lived in the Arctic, the north, and we were in Antarctica, the south. I was extremely glad I hadn't chipped in with my question or I would have looked like a total munter.

Once we got to work I soon came up against a huge challenge:

camping. I'm not a luxury guy, but if I had to go camping on the Coromandel I'd be looking up Airbnb. Part of the documentary involved us spending three nights at Cape Evans, which was where the great adventurer Captain Robert Falcon Scott was based before he died trying to get to the South Pole and back in the 1910s. Sure, I'd have modern-day comforts, but for me, sleeping in a tent in minus 35 degrees Celsius and peeing into a bottle at night would be quite the test. Antarctica has a no-waste rule — including urine. So every visit into the field meant taking a pee bottle. At Camp Evans there was a long-drop, but at night it was way too cold to wander out for a leak. Hence you peed in a bottle, bearing in mind I was sharing my tent with Dom. We're good mates, but having to come to an arrangement about peeing protocols was awkward.

Being at Scott Base was a three-week-long education. My roommate was a brilliant scientist and lovely guy called Professor Craig Cary, from Waikato University. He was hardly ever in his bunk because he was in the field, collecting microbes from the crater of Mount Erebus and testing them in the lab. When he was back at the base, he regaled me with bedtime stories from his dozens of trips to the ice and the adventures he'd enjoyed, and I fell asleep one night as he told me how he'd used a Covid swab to get a poo sample from a penguin's bum.

Craig also taught me an important lesson. I was asking him what the microbes he collected would be useful for: what do we get out of it? He got a bit miffed, and explained his role was pure science, the science of discovery — it was his job to find the microbes, and it was someone else's job to maybe one day figure out if they had a practical use. It was a powerful and inspiring moment, and it hammered home the value of science to me in a whole new way. I listened even more closely to what the scientists had to say about climate change and how it was melting the continent — although I did come up with my own way of thinking about what was going on. Reflecting on the power and beauty of Antarctica, I thought: *Why would we fuck with this?*

”

On the last day of the trip, two guys from Scott Base invited me for a walk up Observation Hill. It was a steep, rocky climb to a spot where the first explorers used to go to look out across Antarctica.

At the top, we could see across the expanse of the continent, the South Pole far beyond; and right behind us was Mount Erebus. There was a big wooden cross, erected here in memory of Captain Scott and his men. We stood in awe, Antarctica all around, in this place of courage and sacrifice. I thought of how I was pushing my personal limits, pushing out the edges of where I saw my career going.

On the cross was a line from Tennyson's poem 'Ulysses'.

'To strive, to seek, to find, and not to yield . . .'

I read it again, and it sunk in: this is me, this is how I want to be.

22. *NEWSHUB* DOWN

After getting back from Antarctica, I put on my penguin suit. Not because I missed the penguins, but because I'd been nominated for Best Presenter: News and Current Affairs at the 2023 New Zealand Television Awards. Karen O'Leary was nominated, too, for Best Presenter: Entertainment, and *Paddy Gower Has Issues* for Best Current Affairs Programme. It was a brilliant result for the show. You'd normally hear a lot of good people say: 'It's not about the awards for me — it's about the work.' I'd love to say that here, but I'm not going to. I'll be honest and say I really wanted to win the presenter award on a whole lot of levels. I'd been nominated for awards a few times before, and always just missed out on the big one.

This was one award I'd really coveted but I dared not imagine I could win. I built it up so much it had become way more than an award. It was a personal symbol of redemption and recognition;

that I was worthy; a validation of the path I'd followed for the past 25 years in journalism, with all the turmoil, doubt, grief and anguish, as well as the triumphs. So there you go: they don't call me the Oversharer-in-Chief for nothing.

Not that I let any of this on to anyone. Instead I just acted weirdly for weeks, pretending it wasn't about the awards for me, that I was all about the work. I even claimed I didn't want to go. When the night rolled around, I was in a class of my own for the award of Most Wound-up Person in New Zealand. I was feeling sicker and sicker as the night wore on, but then Karen won her category, and I felt slightly less sick for about one second, because my category was up next. I was about to puke when Rena Owen read out my name. I was suddenly in a class of my own for the award of Most Stoked Person in New Zealand. It felt good to thank all the people who'd helped me, the people who watched and the people I'd fought for. And there was something to finally square away, someone in particular I needed to thank.

”

As ecstatic as I was about the award, there was a disconcerting vibe about the night. *The Project*, which had helped me make those big changes, had been axed. And it was real niggly that the bosses had only given us verbal assurances regarding the renewal of *PGHI*. And around that time, I'd heard a rumour, from one of those well-placed sources of mine, that there was talk of shutting *Newshub* down.

Jon Bridges pressed the issue with *PGHI*, and just before Christmas got an indication we'd get ten episodes — fewer than we expected, but at least it was something. I'd achieved that goal of getting the show renewed, even if it was what people would call winning ugly. We kicked off 2024 with Jon lining up our team for the new season and getting the contracts drawn up. Then on Friday, 9 February, I was driving home on the motorway when the phone rang. JB was on the line with the outgoing news boss Sarah Bristow and her interim replacement, my old boss Richard Sutherland. They broke the news that *PGHI* was on hold. The twelve people, our close-knit team, who'd turned down other jobs to commit to working with us, needed to be told. One of them was due to start on the Monday. Fuck. JB and I were told what was happening was just a 'pause', that there was a spending freeze but there was hope it would be lifted and we'd be back on track. They were very reassuring. I was not reassured, not one little bit.

Then a meeting was put into our calendars for 28 February, a company-wide, 'all-hands' meeting. We were going to be briefed by James Gibbons, one of the Warner Bros. Discovery bigwigs based in Singapore. The meeting itself wasn't suspicious — there had been other similar ones when WBD gave us updates about what was happening in the wider company, usually around the time annual financial results were released, with Gibbons beaming in via Zoom. So the insinuation was that the 28 February meeting was all good.

But I sensed something wasn't right. Others did, too. The day before, on 27 February, I caught up with my mate Ryan Bridge, whose 7 p.m. current affairs show had also been put on hold. We'd formed what we jokingly called 'The Unemployed Anchors Club', and had a meeting over coffee up the road from the Flower

Street headquarters. Since we had time on our hands, we delved into the darkest recesses of what we could find online about the financial health of WBD globally. Ryan and I discussed our findings, added everything together, and did some back-of-the-envelope maths. We brainstormed every possible outcome, from cutbacks to shut-down. After all that, we concluded: everything would be sweet. There might be some rough economic waters ahead, but it would all work out. We'd be employed anchors soon enough. We parted ways completely calm about the next day's meeting.

I got into work on 28 February, and at 10.04 a.m. we all received a generic message in large, bold, blue letters telling us: 'We ask you to prioritise your attendance at this meeting ahead of everything else you may be doing. The purpose of this meeting is to inform you of some proposed significant changes to the business that may impact your role.' *Fuck.* There were 56 minutes before the meeting. As people always say in these sorts of situations, the 56 minutes seemed very long. Everybody was worried and I could see even the newsroom bosses looked scared.

”

The meeting was at the Dalmatian Cultural Society hall nearby. Strangely, I reverted into political editor mode, and started studying everything like I had at other big announcements over the years, reading the body language and frantically scanning the room for any hints. I was desperate to crack it, to figure it out before the words were actually said. As I walked up the stairs, someone said they'd seen James Gibbons. *We are in serious shit,* I thought. A bigwig like that wouldn't be in town to say gidday. It was either TV3 getting shut down, *Newshub* getting shut down, or a brutal restructure with huge job losses.

The room was set out with a couple of hundred chairs. I sat near the front, and within minutes every seat was taken, with people filling out of every nook and cranny of the Flower Street building. And sure enough, standing there in front of us, next to WBD's New Zealand boss, Glen Kyne, was James Gibbons, the bigwig from Singapore. I'd previously met Gibbons so I nodded hello. He acknowledged me, but didn't smile, not in a rude way, just in a corporate game-face way. *We're fucked*, I thought.

In one of the great, weird ironies, the bosses had an autocue — I couldn't help but smile that they were using a TV prop to help them dish bad news to TV staff. They started the corporate preamble, key words and clichés — economic headwinds, downturns, ad revenue down . . . and on and on. And then Gibbons said: 'The proposed model would see the shutdown of the newsroom.' It was the word 'newsroom' that hit me. He didn't say *Newshub* — which was the brand name. He said 'newsroom'. To journos, the newsroom is a living thing, not just at TV3 but anywhere news is made. I'd been working in newsrooms every day of my working life. I heard gasps first. Then I heard loud sobs. I didn't dare turn around. It was like that moment in a funeral where everyone has been holding on, bracing themselves, and then something has cracked and the tears are unstoppable; heaving, private sorrow in a public space.

I just wanted the bosses to stop. I wanted them to stop reading the fucking autocue. Just as I'd defaulted into political-editor mode, others had fallen into character, too. Michael Morrah, the investigative reporter, fired hard questions. Angus Gillies, the 6 p.m. bulletin producer and newsroom character, cracked a joke: 'Oh, well, we know what tonight's lead story is.' It got the only decent laugh of the meeting. I looked along the row of seats and saw Mike McRoberts. I called him the 'Mighty Tōtara of News'. He was the man we all looked up to in the tough times; he'd been through so much at TV3, through the Weldon years, through previous financial strife — when the company went into receivership in 2013 and when it came within a day of the doors being shut in 2019 before WBD took over — and nothing ever seemed to rattle him . . . But this was beyond all of that. Even Mike McRoberts looked a bit rattled.

The bosses kept talking; it was getting more corporate, more brutal. I was working it all out in my head. My job was gone, my show was gone, my plans were gone. I didn't have time to get sad about how unfair it all was, because right then I heard someone across from me crying, really sobbing. It was camera operator Hannah Warburton. She'd started as an autocue operator and worked her way through the ranks. She was the kind of person I loved working with at *Newshub*, people who'd taken an opportunity and thrived. But she was just starting out. She hadn't had the chance to do the stuff I'd done, and that was truly unfair.

I couldn't reach out to her, to say that she was amazing and should be proud of what she'd done. Seeing Hannah like that, I suddenly felt compelled to speak. Not to the bosses, but to the crew. So I stood up and said I wanted to say something. The bosses looked nervous. I turned around to the room, and for the first time saw the faces of my friends and colleagues, all so sad and frightened. I was taken aback by how many there were. I said to them it was important to remember some amazing people had started making news at TV3 in 1989, and it would be finished off by some amazing people — them. I said that everything was going to get scary as soon as we walked out the doors of the hall and when reality hit, to just stay calm, take a moment, and remember they were amazing and they'd been part of something amazing.

News of what was going on leaked long before the bosses finished their spiel. So many journos around the country had my number so my phone was just bombarded with messages from reporters chasing the story. Even Tony Wall — Wallo, my first journalistic crush — texted. He didn't even say 'hey, sorry to hear . . .' or anything — he just hit me with a question, asking me to confirm if the rumours were true and to text a quote. I appreciated that from Wallo.

”

It was of course a 'proposal', and in the corporate process you were allowed to give 'feedback' that supposedly could reverse the proposal. I was on a committee of seven journos led by Morrah that came up with a radical solution to save some of *Newshub*. It obviously felt like we were battling, and sometimes it felt pointless, but we all agreed to fight to the end because that was the *Newshub* way. We wanted to do it for our colleagues, and everyone who went before us. It was a good idea, and it could have worked for the company. There was a reason for that: we cut the place to the bone. Morrah had to present the idea to our colleagues who'd sent us off to try and save the place. It was awkward as hell given we were proposing cutting a lot of their jobs. I wasn't even going to be part of it myself, but I just wanted to save something, anything, of *Newshub*. The company turned down our proposal. *Newshub* was shutting down. I'd done fourteen years there. I hadn't just lost my job — I'd lost my dreams, and my friends. There was a Rod Emmerson cartoon in the *Herald* the next day with my face on it. It said: 'And That's the ****ing News, Folks!!'

I was interviewed by Mike Hosking on NewstalkZB the next morning, and he asked for my response to those people who were saying 'go woke, go broke', that *Newshub* had collapsed because we were 'woke'. I thought those out there punching down on people who'd lost their jobs were out of line and my emotions got the better of me, and I said they could 'get stuffed'. The truth is I narrowly avoided another on-air f-bomb.

"

There was one particular person I thought of throughout that time of upheaval. Gordon 'Flash' McBride, my old boss in Wellington, the bureau chief who'd done so much to protect me in those dark early days of TV, had died of cancer in 2016. He was one of the people I'd had a chance to thank at that award ceremony when I won Best Presenter: News and Current Affairs. It was something I'd wanted to square away for a long time. He'd been like my work dad and one of my best mates, but I was shocked when his wife, Patricia, rang before the funeral and told me Gordon wanted me to be a pallbearer. It was a real 'who, me?' moment. The cunning bastard had never mentioned it, even though we were having some really good chats near the end. I couldn't believe he'd chosen me to help carry him out, next to his brother and really good mates he'd had for decades. I guess he wanted another journo who could take some of his news values into the future, but I'll never know. It was one of the greatest honours of my life and one I never got to thank him for. So as I got through my acceptance speech and made my way to the end, the time finally came: I dedicated it to Gordon, ending the speech with, 'This one's for you, Flash.' It felt like I'd paid him back. I reckon Gordon would've liked it.

Gordon always believed in me. When he was dying I'd visit him at home or in the hospice and we'd have deep and meaningful yarns like we used to over a bottle of red in his office. One time I was stressed about something at Parliament so I went to see him. He was lying in bed and we started having a chat, and it was so relaxing, I lay down on the ground next to his bed and fell into a sound sleep. When I woke up he cracked up laughing.

We started having a yarn about my future, and Gordon was getting all wise and insightful. I thought, *Here we go, I'd better listen to this*, not wanting to miss a single word.

'You know where I reckon you'll end up?' he said. I couldn't wait to hear what this great newsman would have to say — my own 7 p.m. show? The BBC? CNN? Maybe back at Granny *Herald* as editor? It felt like my future would be decided in this momentous pronouncement.

'I think you'll be the CEO of Fonterra.' I laughed, thinking, *Okay, the drugs have well and truly kicked in.*

”

For the record, as strong as my Taranaki roots are, I have no interest in switching to the dairy business. The big question of course is, with the media so damn fucked-up right now, what does my future hold?

People have even asked if I'd ever go into politics, and if I am left- or right-leaning. In my political reporting I was a complete mercenary — I'd go wherever the controversy was. And being up close to politics, it's become obvious that neither left nor right has all the answers; both sides have good ideas and they definitely both have bad ideas. These days my independence is important to me — I prefer to investigate issues, make people think about them, and suggest solutions where I can. Besides, I spent ten years working in Parliament, the same time as some people spend in Paremoremo serving a life sentence for murder. They are similar places, except there are more psychos in Parliament. Do you ever see people voluntarily going back to Paremoremo? No. So, no, I won't be going into politics, no fucking way.

Continuing on as a journalist might seem a bit fraught. It would be easy for me to get all pessimistic about the state of the media and the global complexities and economic forces that have got us here. I could get all worried about how technology is going to make journos irrelevant anyway. I could say I gave it my all for 25 years and now it is time to give something else a crack.

But I'm a journo, in my brain, heart and soul, and I will find a way to keep going. And when I think back, despite all of the technological changes I've seen, absolutely nothing has changed about how I do the actual job: I connect with people and tell stories. I think of all the Kiwis I've met down the years who've been screwed over in some way, like losing loved ones in traumatic circumstances. I've lost count of the number of times I've walked into someone's house and they've pulled out pages and pages of letters and documents, futile efforts they've made to get to the bottom of what's happened to their son, daughter, brother or sister. Sometimes you could help but sometimes you couldn't — either way, you had to move on to the next story. And I'd just feel like I'd let them down. If I quit the news I reckon I'd feel like that all the time: like I let everybody down.

Somebody has to stick around and be the one who goes up One Tree Hill and brings a bit of history back. Someone has to be down in Parliament giving it to the bastards. Or out in the middle of the debate putting on a big night for New Zealand. Somebody has to help Bernie Monk, or the victims of March 15. Somebody has to be there to help fight for a miracle drug like Trikafta, or help tell the world when the scientists say Antarctica is melting.

So that's why I will keep going.

This is the Fucking News — To Be Continued.

23.
COMING HOME

I love the Taranaki coastline. My favourite beach is Ōakura and just beyond that is Ahu Ahu Road, my favourite surfing spot. Then there are the beaches in town, East End and Fitzroy. Up the coast, beyond Waitara, are the White Cliffs. Each beach is different, its own adventure, with its own memories, its own experiences.

For a lot of people, Taranaki is about the mountain. And that's true for me, too. But this coastline is epic — a big, beautiful, curved line that you can surf any day of the week. The black-sand beaches are pretty rugged, and it's not what everybody wants from a beach, but I quite like that. Taranaki beaches are different, they have their own vibe. Even if you're at one of the beaches in town, you can feel quite isolated, just because they're so wild. It's very easy to feel alone and that's a great feeling. I feel awesome when I get in the waves here, it's like everything else drops away.

Taranaki Mounga itself has that feeling of isolation, and

if you go back to the pūrākau, the legend, of the mountain, it makes sense. Taranaki originally stood near Tūrangi, with Ruapehu, Tongariro and Pihanga. Taranaki and Tongariro both loved Pihanga and fought over her. Eventually, Taranaki stormed off, and on the way, carved the Whanganui River, settling out on his own, away from the other mountains.

And you get that sense when you're here. Taranaki people are resilient and strategic because of that isolation as well. That's why we are just that bit different from everybody else, I reckon. We are outsiders.

"

There's one particular part of the coastline that is the most precious to me. It's at the end of the street I grew up on, so of course that makes it special. There's a spot I like to stand, just under a pōhutukawa tree beside the coastal walkway. If I look to the south, I can see the chimney at the power station where the Old Man worked, and Paritutu Rock, the steep peak by the wharves. If I turn around and look inland, straight up my old street, there's this most perfect view of the mountain, thrusting towards the sky.

It makes me think of the whakatauākī or proverb: 'Whāia te iti kahurangi, ki te tuohu koe, me he maunga teitei.' ('Seek the treasure that you value most dearly, if you bow your head, let it be to a lofty mountain.') It's all about refusing to give in, not letting anything stop you from chasing your dreams. Give it everything. If something's going to stop you, make sure it's something big. Don't fall at the first small challenge.

But the main reason this part of the coastline is precious is that we placed Mum's ashes here. We scattered them in one of the rockpools below. As the tide came in, they were picked up by the water, and I like to stand here and think of how the sea spread them all along the Taranaki coastline.

Mum would walk along the coastal walkway, and when I'm here I can still see her doing that, chatting away. I can also see her on the times she came on my school trips to the rock pools, when we'd hunt for crabs and sea anemones.

I've come here when I've been struggling with my mental health. I've come here to connect. I've come here to remind myself to live with optimism. To work with purpose. To keep control of my life. To change myself if I need to, and to get out there to help make change for people who need it, too.

Most of the time I'll stand by the tree on the clifftop, but if I want to feel closer to Mum I'll climb down to the rockpools. It's not a sad place. I don't talk to Mum or anything like that. It's just a place for a personal pep talk. To remind myself that life is for living, don't waste it.

It's a place for me to reflect, too. I never did much reflecting about anything before my breakdown or while I was still on the booze. I had to figure my issues out, and rebuild myself, create a better Paddy.

This is my tūrangawaewae as far as I'm concerned. This is me. This is where my story comes from. There's no place more special than right here. So when I go, I want to be put here, too. I want to come home.

When I start thinking very deeply when I stand here, I get a feeling that I was put on this earth for a reason, a destiny.

To do things for other people, to do things for Aotearoa New Zealand. To make my mum proud. When my ashes are put in the rockpools down there, I want to go out into the Taranaki sea, at peace, knowing I did all that.

THANKS (VERY F#$%ING MUCH)

I want to give thanks to Eugene Bingham — one of my journalistic heroes since way back in the day. In one of those epic twists that life throws up, he was the 'ghostwriter' of this book. Having him in that role was a privilege, but the bigger privilege is the special friendship it has created. The poor bastard had to listen to a lot — thanks, bro!

Thanks to the team at Allen & Unwin, especially publisher Michelle Hurley, who had the vision and kept at me to push go on this. I'm so stoked I did. I'm not good with deadlines, so a double thanks to project editor Leanne McGregor and copy editor Tracey Wogan for keeping this thing on track and helping make it a banger. Thanks also to photographer Stephen Tilley and designer Kate Barraclough for the epic cover.

Going viral, being in the public eye and using my own issues in my work has meant that sometimes 'This is the Fucking News' becomes more like 'This is Fucking Paddy's Life'. But I haven't shared everything in this book: I have a private life, private family and private friends. I've chosen not to share that stuff for a bunch of reasons, but mostly: That's all I have left. That is the only thing now that's mine and is private. And I hope people respect that. The oversharing stops there. My people know who they are, and no amount of thanks would ever be enough!

And finally, I'd like to thank all the people I work with, the people I fight for, and most of all the people who watch, listen and read. After all, that's what the fucking news is all about.